In December of 1914, veteran Boer commander General Louis Botha landed his forces on the coast of German South West Africa to finish off the colony's *Schutztruppe* defenders. In August, the South Africans had started off badly with a disastrous battle at Sandfontein and an internal rebellion that could have torn the Union of South Africa apart. Botha's campaign would eventually lead to victory, but it would not be easy. Overshadowed and largely forgotten by the battles in Europe, this was one of the more distant and now almost forgotten episodes of World War I. But from August 1914 to July 1915, a small German force of 4,000 faced nearly 75,000 Allied troops of the Union of South Africa, Britain, and colonial Rhodesia in a fight that was pivotal in the history of southern Africa. This loss on the battlefield would cost Germany her most prized African possession and prove to be an important milestone in the history of the country that would eventually become Namibia. Britain was so concerned about the threat the German protectorate of South West Africa posed to the Empire that it requested its dominion, the Union of South Africa, occupy the territory's ports and destroy its powerful wireless stations. South African leaders were eager to take on this 'urgent Imperial service' to expand their own territory.

When the Germans capitulated nearly a year later, it was the first Allied victory of the war and a rallying point for the United Kingdom. It was a terrible place to fight a war. Invading troops wondered why anyone would want to live in the place, let alone fight over it. Vast deserts barred easy entry to the country; the bones of animals and humans scattered across the surface attested to their lethal nature. The South Africans had to feed and water over 100,000 horses and oxen where little fodder existed and after the Germans had sabotaged many of the water points. Meanwhile, the Germans were looking over their shoulders as the native peoples they had long mistreated tried to settle old scores through ambushes and sniping.

Using primary sources, on the ground research, and accurate maps and charts of the battles, the author sheds new light on the operations of the South African Army in its first foreign war and the *Schutztruppe* defense of German South West Africa. The book also demonstrates the terrible cost of miscalculations by politicians and military leaders on both sides.

James Stejskal was born in 1954 in Omaha and grew up on the Great Plains of Nebraska. After trying college, he enlisted in the military and successfully passed assessment and selection to qualify for duty with US Army Special Forces. He served 23 years with Special Forces and special mission units conducting operations in many 'interesting places' worldwide before retiring as a Chief Warrant Officer 4. He then joined the US State Department and served as a diplomat, mostly in Africa, for 11 years, retiring in 2012.

Given his background in military and international political and security affairs, he began to devote more time to historical research and quickly evolved into a military historian. He is the author of a number of articles on military history and conflict archaeology, and holds a Master's Degree in Military Studies and a Bachelor's Degree in History. He works as a consulting historian for the Namib Battlefield Heritage Project, a collaborative effort to record and preserve World War I battle sites in Namibia, and as a conflict archaeologist associated with the Great Arab Revolt Project in Jordan.

He currently lives in Alexandria, Virginia with his wife, Wanda. This is his first book.

THE HORNS OF THE BEAST

THE SWAKOP RIVER CAMPAIGN AND WORLD WAR I IN SOUTH-WEST AFRICA 1914-15

James Stejskal

Helion & Company Ltd

Helion & Company Limited
26 Willow Road
Solihull
West Midlands
B91 1UE
England
Tel. 0121 705 3393
Fax 0121 711 4075
Email: info@helion.co.uk
Website: www.helion.co.uk
Twitter: @helionbooks
Visit our blog http://blog.helion.co.uk/

Published by Helion & Company 2014

Designed and typeset by Farr out Publications, Wokingham, Berkshire
Cover designed by Euan Carter, Leicester (www.euancarter.com)
Printed by Lightning Source, Milton Keynes, Buckinghamshire

ISBN 978 1 909982 78 9

British Library Cataloguing-in-Publication Data.
A catalogue record for this book is available from the British Library.

For details of other military history titles published by Helion & Company Limited contact the above address, or visit our website: http://www.helion.co.uk.

We always welcome receiving book proposals from prospective authors.

Contents

List of illustrations and maps

Illustrations

Maps

Acknowledgments

This book would not have been possible without the encouragement and assistance of a number of people. The expertise and comments of my friend and colleague, Dr John Kinahan of the *Namibian Archaeological Survey*, assisted me to hold a rational course in the retelling of this story. His knowledge of the history, geography, and natural surroundings of the South West were crucial to the interpretation of the physical aspects of the campaign. We spent much time in the field surveying sites and on the veranda discussing the battles, as well as the politics behind them, and this book would not exist without that collaboration. Colonel Mike Phillips, US Army, an old Africa hand, veteran of the Kyber Pass and diplomat, who is eloquent in both history and military analysis, provided insightful comment and critique that has done much to improve my recantation of the story, as well as its concluding analysis. Thanks go to the staffs of the Namibian National Archives, the Western Cape Archives, Botswana National Archives, and the Sam Cohen Library for their assistance in the researching of this work, especially Werner Hillebrecht, the Chief Archivist of the Namibia National Archives who was very helpful to unlocking the secrets of the *Schutztruppe* files in Windhoek. Historian and author Anne Samson provided a most valuable service by reviewing the final draft and giving incisive critique on specific issues, notably British plans and motivations. I would especially like to thank my patient wife, Ambassador Wanda Nesbitt, whose encouragement, along with her incisive reading and commentary, helped immensely in the writing of the work. Finally, I have made all possible effort to locate and acknowledge copyright holders and apologize for any inadvertent infringement. The responsibility for any errors or omissions in this work lies with me alone.

Introduction

This book endeavors to tell the story of a little known aspect of World War I, the South African invasion to seize the German protectorate of South West Africa in the early war years of 1914-1915. The text that follows is primarily concerned with the northern campaign of General Botha that culminated with the German surrender. It only briefly discusses the events, which preceded in the south. Events such as the battle of Sandfontein, disastrous to the initial South African effort to invade the territory, are only generally described as they are ancillary to the main theme. This book attempts to tell the story from the perspective of all the protagonists, South Africa, Britain, Germany and, to a lesser extent, Portugal and Rhodesia.

The goal of this book is to show that the war fought in South West Africa was not just a "side-show" as some attest; the commitment and effort poured into the "overseas" campaigns, as well as the blood and treasure lost, attest to that. Africa was important to Europe and Britain was so concerned about the threat the German colony of South West Africa posed to the Empire that it requested its dominion, the Union of South Africa, to eliminate the German wireless system and occupy the protectorate's harbors. And, although South African leaders were eager to take on this "urgent Imperial service" in order to expand their own territory, it would prove more difficult than initially imagined.

This was a campaign that saw the mobilization of the South African Union Defense Force for its first foreign war, the first deployment of a Royal Naval Armored Car Squadron (equipped with the Rolls-Royce Silver Ghosts) outside Europe, and the first use of aerial bombs in Africa during World War I.

Overshadowed by the horrors of the war in Europe, the South West African campaign was one of the more distant and almost forgotten episodes of World War I. From August 1914 to July 1915, German troops faced the Allied forces of the Union of South Africa, Britain, and the colonial troops of Rhodesia. After a series of short, but intense, engagements and a drawn-out rearguard action, German South West Africa (GSWA) fell to South African forces under the old Boer commander, General Louis Botha. It was considered the first Allied victory of the war and a rallying point for the forces of the United Kingdom. Its conclusion was just the first chapter for South Africa in World War I, as it then turned to the longer, and ultimately more brutal and frustrating campaign in East Africa. The campaign in South West, however, was crucial for the army of South Africa as it went through a steep learning curve in preparation for other deployments in service to the Empire. For the Germans, it now only serves as a vivid counterpoint to the strategy of Colonel Paul von Lettow-Vorbeck in German East Africa.

Although small in scale when compared to the epic battles of the Western Front, the campaign in GSWA was nevertheless pivotal, as it ultimately stripped Germany of its most prized African possession and proved an important milestone in the history of the country that would eventually become Namibia.

This work addresses the British and South African political calculations for the conquest and occupation of colonies Germany initially and naively thought to be neutral and excluded from the conflict raging in Europe.

I have utilized contemporary first and second-hand accounts, official histories, and later works to tell the story of this campaign from the perspectives of all protagonists.

All references are listed in the bibliography, but several are noted here as especially important to the retelling. From the South African perspective, the official history of the campaign, *South Africa in the Great War 1914-1918*, as well as J.J. Collyer's *The Campaign In German South West Africa* were key to following the campaign. From the German side, Oelhafen's *Der Feldzug in Südwest 1914 – 1915*, Richard Hennig's *Deutsch-Südwest im Weltkrieg*, and von Seitz's *Südafrika im Weltkrieg* were crucial. Von Seitz's work is also important to understand his perception of the Allied motivations for the invasion. The official German history, *Der Feldzug in Deutsche Südwestafrika, 1914-1915*, exists only as a draft written by the German General Staff's Historical Research Department in 1943, but it is valuable for its critique of the *Schutztruppe* leadership, tactics, and discussion of the campaign in general.

More contemporary works like Gerald L'Ange's *Urgent Imperial Service* are useful, but like von Seitz, they are often biased in outlook. L'Ange's claim that Germany bore the lion's share of blame for the invasion, for example, fails to acknowledge the underlying Allied motivations that are clearly outlined in the papers of the British and South African leadership. Scholarly works such as those by Matthew Seligmann and Anne Samson are also used in my analysis of this campaign.

Additionally, previous documentary accounts of the campaign lack detail of the actual sites involved; it is only through recent archaeological field surveys conducted in 2011 through 2013 that the course of events can be securely placed in the landscape.

This book tells the history of a nearly forgotten campaign in a remote corner of Africa and the sacrifices made for Empire in a war that took place nearly 100 years ago.

The enemy? His sense of duty was no less than yours, I deem. You wonder what his name is, where he came from. And if he was really evil at heart. What lies or threats led him on this long march from home. If he would not rather have stayed there in peace. War will make corpses of us all.

J.R.R. Tolkein, *The Lord of the Rings*

Prologue

The causes of World War I were myriad and complex. Although competition for colonial assets is often cited as one of numerous catalysts, few governments thought war would actually be fought on battlefields away from Europe. In 1914, the British Empire comprised one quarter of the world with the dominions of Canada, South Africa, Australia, New Zealand, as well as British India, the colony of British East Africa and the chartered territory of Southern Rhodesia in its realm. Germany, on the other hand, came to the colonial game much later and possessed only four protectorates in Africa: Togo, Cameroon, German East Africa and South West Africa.[1] German *Reichschancellor* Otto von Bismarck, a proponent of rational politics, cautioned that colonies would cost more than they were worth and his admonition proved true. After Bismarck was dismissed in 1890, Kaiser Wilhelm II began to put in place an aggressive *Weltpolitik* that aimed to make Germany a global player. Confrontation would replace rationalism. Germany's policies, its naval expansion, and its colonial possessions became a threat to Britain's Empire. Whereas France and Russia were Britain's rivals at the end of the 19th Century, Germany replaced them in the 20th.[2]

Few European colonial settlers in Africa believed the coming war would affect them and most thought the conflict, when it did come, would be fought between the great nations on the battlefields of Europe. The colonies were thought to be immune – neutral territories that were neither to take part in the battle nor be attacked by the warring parties.

One and one half times larger than Germany itself, German South West Africa (GSWA) had begun to be a productive colony for the fatherland. Diamonds had been discovered in 1908, which brought more settlers seeking fortune, if not fame. By 1914, there were around 13,000 Germans (and a few "foreigners") living in the protectorate, the largest number of any of its colonies. This compared to an estimated 135,000 native peoples.

The presence of settlers, most of whom lived as ranchers and traders, had caused conflict with the indigenous peoples from their arrival. Numerous small skirmishes and two ugly internal revolts were fought ending with the suppression of the 1904-1908 Herero and Namaqua (Nama) uprisings and the deaths of between 30,000 and 70,000 indigenous men, women, and children. The wars were costly, however, and the German government had reduced its expenditures by drastically cutting the size of the colony's security force, leaving only a force suitable for internal stability. In 1914, the country had been at peace for six years and most Germans settlers wished it would remain that way.

---

1   At the beginning of the war, Germany also possessed colonies in the Pacific including German New Guinea and Samoa, as well as the Chefoo and Kiautschou Bay concessions.
2   Matthew Seligmann details the background of Anglo-German colonial rivalry in his book, *Rivalry in Southern Africa: The Transformation of German Colonial Policy*.

Südwest as it was often referred to in Germany, spawned many rough and tumble books such as Gustav Frenssen's *Peter Moor's Journey to Southwest Africa*. These stories, like Karl May's exotic tales of North Africa and the American "Wild West", often led young boys and men who read them to dream about the seemingly adventurous and potentially rewarding life of the colonies, regardless of how distorted those views were. In reality, it was a place where the wagons of the Boer *voortrekkers* and German *Siedler* penetrated a difficult, hostile environment while warring natives resisted the foreign invader encroaching on their homelands. There were good and bad aspects to both sides, but ignorance, fear, and an overriding feeling of racial superiority infused the psyche of many settlers and soldiers who came to the territory. In the end, as in the novels, the indigenous peoples would lose to Western "civilization".

In 1914, much wildness remained in the land. The Germans had finally gained control of much of the territory with the exception of Ovamboland – the far north where the threat of hostile natives and tropical disease kept most Europeans at bay. But even in the southern "pacified" territory known as the Police Zone, the environment was hard. Harsh desert made up much of the land and drought made daily life difficult in the rest. Many Germans wondered why anyone would want to fight over such a territory.

But war would come. Because Germany's colonies sat astride important sea-lanes, they were a threat to England's imperial trade and commerce. The huge Telefunken radio transmitters located at Kamina, Togo and Windhoek allowed direct communication with the world's largest radio site at Nauen in Germany. They were used by the Kaiser's Navy to relay information around the world and, thus, threatened the Royal Navy's supremacy. They were built because Germany correctly anticipated England would seek to control the undersea telegraph cables at the outset of any war. One of England's first military moves in 1914 would be to cut the cables linking Germany to the outside world and try to destroy her colonial wireless stations by naval bombardment.[3]

Although the origins of World War I did not lie primarily in colonial rivalry, the colonies played a role in the war. Germany did not want her colonies to be involved and erroneously believed the Berlin Treaty of 1885 made them neutral entities. England, however, had few reservations to extending the war beyond Europe.

Germany's colonial military commanders in Africa knew they could not win the war on the continent, but once the conflict came they hoped to hold out until a German victory in Europe saved them. Most knew that defeat in Europe would end their colonial aspirations once and for all. Some felt they could help the overall war effort by forcing the Allies to divert blood and treasure to fighting in the colonies. In German East Africa, they largely succeeded. Allied forces invaded the German colonies in the Pacific and West Africa early in the war. The last to fall would be German East Africa in November 1918. Between those events, German South West Africa would provide a battleground over which two mismatched armies would be pitted against each other in a campaign that lasted almost a year.

The campaign in South West Africa was small compared with the war in Europe. At its conclusion, the lives that were changed were largely those of the European settlers. World War I was a "white man's war" fought for "European" objectives. Little of the country was

---

3   One of the few overseas cables left intact passed through England and was monitored by British intelligence. This allowed the British to intercept the so-called Zimmermann Telegram that brought the United States into the war.

damaged and relatively few lives, indigenous or European, were lost. Those, which were lost, belonged mostly to the whites.

When the surrender was signed in July 1915, a lot would change in South West Africa, but much would be the same. For the Germans, their world was turned upside down while the South Africans had won a territory they had long coveted and over which they would rule for the next seventy-two years. For the indigenous peoples, a hope that freedom would come drove many to assist the South Africans, but was quickly dashed. They had gone from the frying pan to the fire and would be compelled to fight again and again to win independence.

The campaign that took place in South West Africa is largely forgotten today, overshadowed by the greater war in Europe and the longer battle for East Africa with its charismatic German commander Colonel Paul von Lettow-Vorbeck. Additionally, neither the current governments of Namibia nor South Africa care to remember the campaign or celebrate its end. For the majority of the citizens of these countries, it is merely one more event in the long history of "imperialist oppression" that ended for Namibia in 1990.

Nevertheless, World War I in Africa was a pivotal event in the history of the continent. War changed the face of Africa and ushered in the end of one phase of colonialism while beginning another. The war was an important part of the history of South Africa and Namibia as it set the stage for a long struggle that would be waged to secure dignity and freedom for all peoples.

Dramatis Personæ

Union of South Africa

General Louis Botha. Prime Minister and one of the country's most competent and respected military commanders. He pursued an asymmetrical and largely conventional offensive to seize German South West Africa (GSWA) in 1915. Following the allied victory, Botha attended the 1919 Versailles Peace Conference and passed away the same year.

Colonel (later Brigadier) Coen Brits. Led Botha's left wing during the campaign in German South West Africa and later served in East Africa.

Colonel (later Brigadier) John Johnston 'JJ' Collyer. Served as Botha's Chief of Staff during the war and was responsible for coordinating the operations of an army little experienced in combined operations. A chief architect of the Defense Act of 1912 and, after the war, he wrote much of the official history of Union Defense Force (UDF) operations in GSWA and East Africa. Collyer was also the author of many of the UDF's early manuals on operations and tactics.

Colonel (later Lieutenant General) Jacob van Deventer, KCB. A brigade commander under General Botha, later Commander in Chief of Allied forces in East Africa.

General Jan Christiaan Smuts. As Minister of Defense, Smuts was responsible for the initial planning to invade the German protectorate. After the campaign he served in German East Africa as Commander in Chief of the allied forces. He went on to serve in various positions with the South African Government including prime minister.

Germany

Lieutenant Colonel Carl Erich Anton Victor Franke. Became commander of the *Schutztruppe* following the death of Joachim von Heydebreck. He commanded in GSWA through to the surrender in July 1915.

Lieutenant Colonel Joachim von Heydebreck. A career army officer who became *Schutztruppe* commander in 1912 and engineered the initial defense of GSWA. He was fatally wounded during the test firing of a new rifle grenade at Kalkfontein-Süd in November 1914.

Captain (later General) Paul Emil von Lettow-Vorbeck. Adjutant and Company Commander under General Trotha in GSWA during the 1904-1908 Herero and Namaqua uprisings, later commander of German forces in German East Africa (GEA) from 1914-1918.

Governor Theodor von Seitz. In 1910 he was appointed Governor of German South West Africa (GSWA) and served until the surrender of the German forces. Von Seitz ordered the mobilization in early August 1914 and led the surrender negotiations in July 1915.

General Lothar von Trotha. German commander who ruthlessly suppressed the Herero and Namaqua uprisings in GSWA, 1904-1908. Also served during the Boxer Rebellion in China and the Wahehe uprising in GEA.

Captain Rüdiger Weck, A General Staff Officer, Weck served as the *Schutztruppe*'s Chief of Staff and was responsible for formulating and disseminating Heydebreck's, then Franke's operational plans for the German forces until his death in April 1915, the result of a fall from his horse. He was succeeded by Captain Georg Trainer.

Britain

Lieutenant Colonel (later Colonel) Frederick Trench, DSO. Artillery officer and military attaché to the German commander in GSWA, 1905-1906, and at the British Embassy in Berlin, 1906-1910.

Lieutenant Commander W. Whittal. Naval officer and Commander of Number 1 Squadron, Royal Naval Air Service Armored Car Division in GSWA and later in GEA.

1

Origins of a Conflict

It was 1914 and the clouds of war were gathering over German South West Africa. Although the conflict that would play out in the protectorate was small given the scale of the Great War in Europe and elsewhere, it was key to the Allies' African campaign and the history of the country that would eventually become Namibia. The participants included a small German colonial military force defending the territory against a much larger army fielded mainly by the Union of South Africa with some British and Rhodesian attachments. Indigenous peoples such as the Bastar, Herero, and Namaqua would also serve as guards, scouts, drovers, forced labor, and sometimes insurgents during the war. In the end, it was the South Africans who would benefit more from the use of indigenous support forces. The Germans, having quashed two recent revolts, had few armed indigenous troops in its service and feared arming or using any of the restive tribes in a conflict against fellow Europeans, primarily because the feared a resurgence of violence against their own people. Prior to World War I, the Germans believed the British were supporting rebels inside the protectorate, a belief they would carry over into the 1914-1915 conflict.[1] The overall Allied victory in 1918 ended German colonial rule in Africa and brought about a new epoch in the history of what is now the country of Namibia.

At the beginning of the 20th Century, the territory of *Deutsche Südwest-Afrika* or German South West Africa (GSWA) was one of four German colonies on the African continent – the others being Togo, Cameroon, and *Deutsche Ost-Afrika* or German East Africa (GEA).[2] Commercially administered by the German Colonial Society for South West Africa (*Deutsche Kolonialgesellschaft für Südwest-Afrika*) since 1884, the Imperial German Government took full control of the protectorate in 1890. From that moment until the surrender of German forces in July 1915, the German Colonial Office administered the protectorate.

GSWA was the only one of the German colonies in Africa that was settled by a sizeable number of Germans. In 1914, the German population in the protectorate numbered about 12,000, while around 2,000 Boer-Afrikaners and less than 1,000 British civilians lived there. According to a rough census conducted in 1902, the indigenous population was about 200,000, but a large proportion, as many as 40,000 to 70,000 men, women, and children perished as a consequence of the fierce Herero and Namaqua (Hottentot) uprisings of 1904-1908.[3]

That war between Britain and Germany would come was a theme that had dominated

---

1   During the 1904-1908 uprisings in GSWA, the British took great pains to ensure their territories were not used as safehavens by insurgents and disarmed any border crossers. They also feared indigenous uprisings in their own colonies. See especially the correspondence between the Regional Magistrates of Bechuanaland and the High Commissioner of the Cape Colony, Botswana National Archives (BNA) RC 11/1 & RC 11/2.
2   German East Africa (GEA) would later become the countries of Tanganyika, Burundi, and Rwanda.
3   The actual numbers and the circumstances behind the deaths continue to be bitterly disputed.

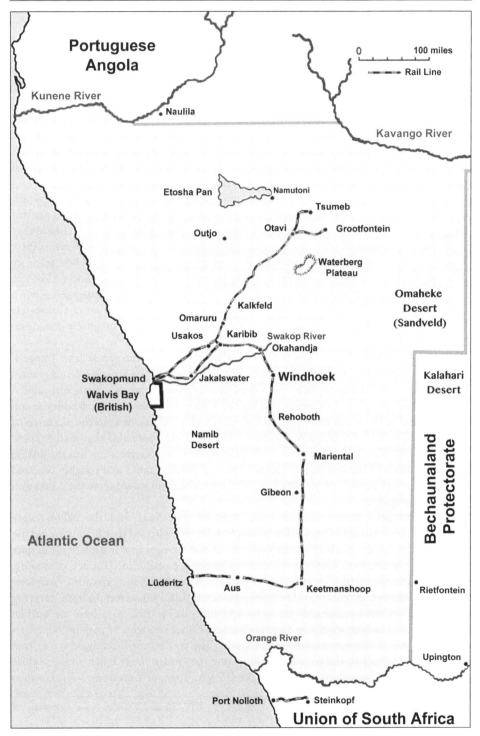

Portuguese Angola

Kunene River

Naulila

Kavango River

0   100 miles

Rail Line

Etosha Pan   Namutoni

Tsumeb

Outjo   Otavi   Grootfontein

Waterberg Plateau

Omaheke Desert (Sandveld)

Kalkfeld

Omaruru

Usakos   Karibib   Swakop River
Okahandja

Swakopmund   Jakalswater   Windhoek

Walvis Bay (British)

Kalahari Desert

Rehoboth

Namib Desert

Mariental

Gibeon

Atlantic Ocean

Bechaunaland Protectorate

Lüderitz   Aus   Keetmanshoop   Rietfontein

Orange River

Upington

Port Nolloth   Steinkopf

Union of South Africa

GSWA 1914 (© James Stejskal)

both private government and public discussion in the early 1900s. On a lesser level, the fear that a war would involve the Cape Colony (Union of South Africa from 1910) and German South West Africa was a subject that had concerned diplomats and military attachés since the Anglo-Boer War (also known as the Second Boer War of Independence or South African War). Mistrust was rampant on both sides of the border, although the Boer who lived in either country probably distrusted the British more. In Europe as well as the colonies, the Germans bristled over Edward VII's *Einkreisungspolitik* – the isolation and containment of Germany by the Entente Powers, while Britain spoke of the Kaiser's bellicose policies, especially Germany's decision to build a navy that would compete with the Royal Navy's dominance of the high seas, the construction of the Berlin-to-Baghdad railway, and two international crises over Morocco in 1905 and 1911.

While British leaders distrusted Germany's global aspirations, the Union of South Africa government was worried about the intentions of its German neighbor. The ill-advised Kruger Telegram in which the Kaiser voiced his support for the Boer in 1896 should they go to war still resonated with leaders in London and Pretoria and made them suspect Germany's territorial ambitions. German missionaries who lived inside Union territory were suspected of being spies and of attempting to mobilize the indigenous peoples to rise in rebellion. The threat of a German invasion of South Africa – real or imagined – was a topic that periodically came up in government circles as well as in the press. Conversely, the threat of war in Europe ensured the Germans in the protectorate maintained an equal distrust of their southern neighbor.

A small military force known as *Die Kaiserlichen Schutztruppen* (the Imperial Protection Force), along with an even smaller police force, *Der Kaiserlichen Landespolizei*, watched over internal security matters in the German protectorate, but being surrounded by Portuguese Angola to the north and by the Union of South Africa, Rhodesia, and Bechuanaland to the south and east, the Germans had few illusions as to the weakness of their position should war come. Additionally, Great Britain controlled the small Atlantic port enclave of Walvis Bay – known as *Walfischbucht* to the Germans – located just 35 kilometers south of the inadequate German port of Swakopmund and roughly centered on GSWA's long coastline. Walvis had an excellent harbor and would serve the Allies well during the campaign.

Both the protectorate Governor Dr Theodor von Seitz and the *Schutztruppe* commander, Lieutenant Colonel Joachim von Heydebreck assessed that Britain would use South African forces to attack the protectorate if and when war was declared – despite Berlin's trust in the 1885 General Act of the Conference of Berlin. This act, commonly called the "Treaty of Berlin", stated that in the case of war between signatories, territories belonging to the belligerents would be considered neutral and would refrain from "carrying on hostilities in the neutralized territories and from using them as a base for warlike operations". As a consequence, the German Foreign Office thought, or perhaps hoped, its territories would be immune to the coming war.[4] The treaty stated clearly, however, that it was applicable only to the territories comprising the Congo River Basin and, therefore, did not apply to other colonies in Africa like GSWA, Togo, or Cameroon.[5] The German

---

4   Hans von Oelhafen, *Der Feldzug in Südwest 1914 – 1915,* 10 and Theodor Seitz, *Südafrika im Weltkrieg,* p.26.

5   While the treaty did apply to German East Africa, Britain's decision to attack the colony was primarily to ensure its command of the seas. Its intent was not (initially, at least) to secure new territory. Additionally,

Lieutenant Colonel von Heydebreck and the *Schutztruppe* staff riding through
veld during maneuvers in August 1914. (© Namibian National Archives)

assumption was wrong and Berlin's refusal to understand this fact left Governor von Seitz
with very limited resources with which to defend the territory. Von Seitz and his commander
were to secure the huge territory with a largely hostile, indigenous population and prepare
for a possible invasion by an external enemy, missions that the Germans were not prepared
to carry out without reinforcements from the fatherland. Von Seitz had consulted in detail
with Heydebreck and previous commanders about the available options as they watched
the threat of war with England grow. As a result, von Seitz – although failing to obtain
approval for an increase in the *Schutztruppe* – did secure passage of a new defense law in
1913 that gave him extensive powers in the event of an emergency. In the spring of 1914, von
Seitz began to put the law into effect. This included the emergency call-up of all reservists,
home defense militia, and those furloughed from active service. He was also authorized to
engage volunteers and recall retired officers to duty.

Shortly after the declaration of war in August 1914, South African Prime Minister
Louis Botha cabled London and stated that the Union Defense Force (UDF) was capable of
independently defending South African territory from German aggression and suggested
the British forces stationed there might be withdrawn for service in Europe. The British
government quickly accepted the offer on 6 August 1914, but requested the government of
South Africa consider undertaking "a great and urgent Imperial service" by seizing GSWA's
port cities of Swakopmund and Lüderitzbucht (Lüderitz Bay) and the wireless stations

although Belgium wanted to keep the colonies out of the war, Britain's bombardment of the wireless
station at Dar es Salaam on 8 August 1914 made the war in Africa a *fait accompli*. On the other hand, the
German commander Lieutenant Colonel von Lettow-Vorbeck wanted very much to draw Britain into
battle over the territory, while the Governor von Schnee wanted to remain neutral. Von Schnee would
lose out to his more bellicose subordinate.

Generals Botha and Smuts during the First World War.
(South African Government Photo – released into Public Domain)

Telefunken Radio Station Windhoek, masts and buildings,
1914. (© Namibian National Archives)

there and in the interior at Windhoek.[6] On 10 August 1914, after consulting with his close colleagues, Botha decided to take on the task and quietly began preparations to mobilize the army for war, a decision that would have serious consequences in the coming months.

The Union Army, along with elements from Britain and British Rhodesia, would launch a campaign to capture the German protectorate with the aim of neutralizing the ports and, more importantly, destroy the large wireless station in Windhoek that was crucially important for German naval raiders and commercial shipping. At the time, the German wireless stations at Kamina, Togo and Windhoek were second only to the Telefunken site at Nauen, Germany, the largest in the world, and all were crucial communication components for the German Imperial Navy and its commercial maritime enterprise.

There were opponents to Botha's course of action; primarily the Boers who had only recently fought against the British Empire in their failed wars of independence. Many of them had taken Boer General Louis Botha at his word when in 1901 he said of the peace agreement with England:

> It is better now to make peace and save what there is to save, before the entire nation is in a concentration camp or murdered by the indigenous peoples. We can take up arms again when Britain is in difficulty and then win our lost freedom.[7]

By 1914, however, Botha's position towards England had softened, while that of many of his countrymen had not. Coupled with internal political bickering over labor issues, this dispute led to a deepening of the schism between those who wanted to support England and those who wanted to rebel. Botha and his close ally and Defense Minister General Jan Christiaan Smuts were on one side; the "old Boers", General J.B.M. Hertzog, Nicolaas de Wet, and former Orange Free State President Martinus Steyn were on the other. Hertzog's National Party opposed Botha's plan and General J.H. del la Rey, following the South African Parliament's 15 September 1914 vote to invade German South West Africa, called the Boer peoples into open rebellion against the government. While much of the UDF was fixed on the border with the Germans, the internal revolt would initially occupy Botha inside South Africa. Botha decided to use loyal Boer troops to fight the Boer rebels. In the end, the Boer uprising was little more than a temporary inconvenience for Botha. Luckily for the government, the majority of the Boers had already reconciled themselves to living within the British Empire.

---

6   Byron Farwell, *The Great War in Africa, 1914-1918*, p.77.
7   Botha's speech at Vereeniging, 7 March 1901.

2

The Forces

South Africa

At the beginning of World War I, South Africa's fledgling army had yet to be tested in battle. It was a force made up of men of Cape Dutch "Boer" and of English descent, an amalgamation of Boer *commando* and colonial volunteer regiments. By any measure though, both groups knew how to fight; this they had proven in the 1st and 2nd Anglo-Boer Wars.

Following the creation of the Union of South Africa in 1910 as a dominion of the United Kingdom, its Prime Minister, General Louis Botha, wanted a "real army" capable not only of fighting a "little Kaffir war" but one able to defend South Africa from any threat.[1] Botha wanted to have an army on a par with those of Europe. The Union Defense Force (UDF) was created under the Defense Act of 1912, written largely by Botha's future Chief of Staff, then Captain J.J. Collyer. The new force was organized on British lines; the old Boer Republic volunteer *commandos* were transformed into the "Active Citizen Force" (ACF) and "Coast Garrison Force" – a total of around 25,000 volunteers, while the core of the UDF was the "Permanent Force" of five regiments of the South African Mounted Riflemen (SAMR) each with an attached artillery battery.

South African Union Defense Force Structure[2]

Prior to 1912	After 1912
Cape Mounted Riflemen	Permanent Force
Cape Mounted Police	10,000 Officers & other ranks
5 Mounted Regiments	
5 Artillery Batteries	
Boer Volunteer Corps	Active Citizen Force / Coast Garrison Force
Militia	25,000 Volunteers
Cadet Corps	16 Mounted Rifle Regiments
12 Dismounted Rifle Regiments	
12 Infantry Battalions	
6 Artillery Batteries	
Rifle Associations	Rifle Associations
	42,000 Volunteers

The Permanent Force (PF) was a constabulary force like its predecessor, the Cape Mounted Riflemen, and required significant augmentation for the war. While the PF had many South Africans of English heritage from the former Cape and Natal colonies, the ACF manned mostly with Afrikaners (native-born South Africans of Dutch descent)

---

1   Botha, Louis, quoted in "The South African Defense Act." *The Morning Post*, 2 July 1912, quoted in *Scientiae Militaria*, Volume 28, Issue 2, September 1998.

2   WA Dorning, "A Concise History of the South African Defense Force (1912-1987)," *Scientia Militaria*, Vol 17, No 2.

from the Orange Free State and Transvaal republics. It was because of Prime Minister Botha's leadership that the UDF was able to mobilize these two disparate groups, the Boer-Afrikaner and the English, who had only twelve years earlier been enemies. But despite Botha's leadership, the initial stages of the war were marked by internal dissent and a rebellion that could have destroyed the new dominion.

The structure of the Boer *commando* and British regiments was quite similar and heavily reliant on familial and community allegiances, although the Boer system was perceived to be less disciplined than its counterpart. Both elements had existed in the Cape Colony and Boer Republics and, upon unification in 1912, were absorbed into the new UDF and would continue to exist side-by-side until the 1980s.[3]

A final component of the UDF was the "Rifle Associations" that constituted the reserve force. Military service was obligatory for all males of European descent from the age of 17 to 60 and personnel were expected to participate in annual military exercises to maintain proficiency. Indigenous South Africans, that is persons not of "European descent" could not volunteer, but about 30,000 were pressed into service as labor forces.

Although many Afrikaners felt the new army imposed British Imperial structure over their traditional ways, the *commando*, the key component of the old Afrikaner militia, and its irregular tactics remained an integral part of the UDF.[4] Historically, a *commando* functioned like a volunteer militia and every able-bodied *Burgher* (citizen) was required to serve. Led by an elected *Kommandant*, the *Burghers* were fiercely independent; each provided his own horse and kit, usually civilian clothing and whatever weapon was at hand. To a far greater extent than in the British Army, discipline was often an issue. Boer *commando* tactics were unconventional, usually improvised while on the move.

The *commandos* relied on speed and surprise, coupled with excellent horsemanship and marksmanship to overwhelm their enemy. Operating as mounted infantry, the *commandos* often attacked en masse to get within rifle range and then dismounted to close with and destroy the enemy. Brave and reckless at the same time, a *commando* in action resembled a group of ill-disciplined ruffians to British officers who were used to ordered structure and movement. And although their tactics were often "rag-tag" and appeared aggressively reckless, the Boers were not averse to retreating to fight another day when the action got too hot. During the Anglo-Boer wars, British officers often refused to alter their tactics in the face of what they considered "ungentlemanly ways of war" and they often suffered heavily when they could not adapt to the unorthodox tactics that confronted them.

The UDF was logistically challenged at the beginning of the war and would rely on the Royal Navy for maritime transport. The hostile natural environment of German South West Africa (GSWA) dictated that supplies, especially food, water, and fodder be moved to Lüderitzbucht or Walvis Bay from Cape Town by ship and thence by wagon, rail, or truck to the front. This necessitated the rebuilding of the German railway system to Cape Gauge and the import of around 2,000 supply trucks to service the logistical requirements of the army. UDF war diaries are replete with details on logistical problems, but none is more illustrative than a comment in one status report that stated: "the heavy artillery could not move; the soldiers had eaten the draft oxen."[5] In the end, many of these problems would be

---

4   A *commando* corresponded roughly to a company-sized element and consisted of around 300 mounted riflemen.
5   J.J. Collyer, *The Campaign In German South West Africa*, p.86.

South African Commando with Lee Enfield rifle – 1914. (© Namibian National Archives)

South African soldier of the Transvaal Scottish Regiment – 1915. (© Namibian National Archives)

overcome by the South African ability to mobilize far greater resources than the Germans could muster.

In 1914, the army's Short Magazine Lee Enfield (SMLE) rifles were being upgraded to use with the new .303 Mark VII ammunition, which forced the issue of the Model 1904 Mauser-Verguiero 6.5mm caliber rifle to the ACF. The Imperial Government received some 20,000 of these rifles from the Portuguese and provided them to the UDF, as the new SMLEs were in short supply everywhere in the Empire. Unfortunately, the Mauser-Verguiero was a fragile rifle and the 12 million rounds of ammunition acquired with the rifles often had cracked cartridge cases or bullets that simply fell out with normal handling.[6] A number of units were issued the older Lee Enfield rifle, mostly in the southern theater. The UDF also had a number of machine-gun detachments equipped with water-cooled Maxims in .303 caliber and a few Danish Madsens.

Several types of artillery were available, including Quick Firing (QF) 13-pounder guns, six QF 12-pounder 18 cwt naval guns, two QF 4.7 inch naval guns modified for land use as heavy artillery, and two 15-pounder Breech Loading Converted (BLC) guns that were

6   J.L. Keene, "The Problem of Munitions Supply in the First World War and its effect on the Union Defense Force", *Military History Journal*, Vol 6 No 4.

South African Field Artillery, with their BL QF 15-pdr
Gun – 1915. (© Namibian National Archives)

South African BLC 15-pdr anti-aircraft gun "Skinny Liz" and crew,
one with heliograph. (© Namibian National Archives)

Henri Farman aircraft of the South African Aviation Corps piloted by LT Kenneth van der Spuy. (© Scientific Society Swakopmund (Incorporated Association – not for Gain)

modified for duty as anti-aircraft guns.

Other elements that served alongside the UDF were the Royal Naval Air Service Armored Car Squadron Number 1 (RNAS No.1), equipped with twelve Rolls-Royce Armored Cars mounting water-cooled Vickers .303 machine-guns, and the 1st Rhodesian Regiment, a 500-man strong infantry formation equipped with Lee Enfield and SMLE rifles, and machine-guns whose troops were all white settlers from the territory. The South African Air Corps came into being on 29 January 1915 and was able to support General Botha using six Henri Farman F-27 and two BE2C aircraft that provided reconnaissance and conducted some bombing missions in the final stages of the war.[7]

Indigenous troops played a significant role in the campaign as well. These little-honored troops served mostly in non-combatant capacities as drovers, cooks, railway workers, and laborers. Many, however, served as scouts and couriers in areas were whites would be hard-pressed to operate. Although General Smuts declined requests by the indigenous peoples to fight because it was a "white man's war", thousands of Blacks and coloreds (mixed-race) men did serve and were important to the final victory.[8]

When war did come, the UDF's organization was found wanting. For example, there was no Commander in Chief designated to lead the army. In August 1914, that responsibility fell to Minister of Defense General J.C. Smuts who was not as talented a military leader as Botha in the field, but did excel on the political stage. Further, the headquarters element lacked a Chief of the General Staff to coordinate planning for the conduct of operations; instead there were three executive commanders who advised the Minister of Defense. There were few trained staff officers and, because of this, there were no plans for the defense of the Union or future contingencies that might arise. Recently promoted to colonel, J.J. Collyer would fill this role for Generals Smuts and Botha throughout World War I. What is more, few of the South African commanders in 1914 were experienced in leading large elements in combined operations. While the UDF's small unit capabilities were good, its ability to

---

7   JOEO Mahncke, "Aircraft Operations In The German Colonies: 1911-1916. The Fliegertruppe of the Imperial German Army", *Military History Journal*, Vol 12 No 2.

8   J.S. Mohlamme, "Soldiers Without Reward: Africans in South Africa's Wars", *Military History Journal*, Vol 10 No 1. Black volunteers were not accepted into the UDF until 1916, after the campaign for GSWA had concluded.

A Rolls Royce armored car of RNAS No 1 Armoured Car Squadron
at Walvis Bay, March 1915. (© Namibian National Archives)

South African 4" naval gun at Tschaukaib – 1915. (© Scientific Society
Swakopmund (Incorporated Association – not for Gain)

conduct larger operations was often hampered by a lack of planning and staff, as well as poor communications and coordination between elements.[9]

Germany

The mission of the *Kaiserlichen Schutztruppe* (Imperial Protection Force) in German South West Africa (GSWA) was to protect white settlers from the territory's indigenous peoples and ensure the internal security of the colony.[10] The *Schutztruppe* was a separate military organization under the auspices of the Colonial Office. Most of its rank and file soldiers came from the enlistment of civilians, many of whom came to the colony having few options back home. The quality of volunteers was often much lower than in the Imperial Army and training was often not thorough. Most officers and some non-commissioned officers were volunteers who elected to serve overseas to improve their promotion prospects and for the adventure of serving in exotic locations overseas.

While Europe was ramping up to war, the German administration in SWA was trying to do more with less. From a high of over 20,000 soldiers manning 23 companies of mounted infantry, artillery, and combat support elements in 1905, the *Schutztruppe* had been reduced to an active strength of less than 2,000 soldiers following the end of the indigenous rebellions. The governor of the protectorate, Dr. Theodor von Seitz had long argued for additional men and modern equipment to provide for the defense of GSWA without success. During a visit to Berlin in 1913, officials within the Colonial Office reminded the Governor that the *Schutztruppe* was not meant to defend the territory against an outside invader.[11]

In August 1914, the *Schutztruppe* stood at 1,967 active officers and other ranks organized in nine mounted infantry companies (one on camels),[12] four full and one half artillery battery, and two *Verkehrszüge* (armored train detachments).[13] By September, after mobilization, the figure reached nearly 5,800 or roughly 60 percent of the available men in the protectorate, but this was effectively reduced to around 4,800 by medical and administrative disqualifications within one month. Even then, only 50 percent of the total was judged suitable for front-line combat operations.[14] The 534 officers and men of *der Kaiserlichen Landespolizei*, the protectorate's police, were integrated into the *Schutztruppe* for wartime duty. Only a small number remained on police duty.

9   Collyer, p.255.
10   The *Schutztruppe* in Germany's other colonies had similar missions. Jürgen Kraus and Thomas Müller, *Die deutschen Kolonial- und Schutztruppen von 1889 bis 1918: Geschichte, Uniformierung und Ausrüstung*, p.222.
11   Richard Hennig, *Deutsch-Südwest im Weltkrieg*, p.34.
12   Gerald L'Ange stated the Germans had a 500-man camel corps. According to *Schutztruppe* records, there was one camel company of around 110 riders.
13   *Hauptquartier der ST, Merkblatt für die Mobilmachung der Schutztruppe für S.W.A.*, ZBU 2372.
14   *Kriegsgeschichtliche Forschungsanstalt des Heeres* (KFH), *Der Feldzug in Deutsche Südwestafrika, 1914-1915*, p.20.

Schutztruppe soldier on horseback (Reiter A. Brade) – 1915. (© Namibian National Archives)

German *Schutztruppe* Field Organization[15]
September 1914
Regiment Bauzus
    1 Company
    3 Artillery Batteries
Regiment Ritter
    3 Companies
    1 Artillery Battery
Regiment Franke
    3 Companies
    1 Artillery Battery
Regiment von Rappard
    2 Companies
Coastal and Border Defense
    3 Companies
    2 Detachments
    Half Artillery Battery
Total Strength: 1,967 officers and men

Schutztruppe Reiter (troopers) were equipped with the Mauser *Gewehr* 98 and 98S rifle in 7.92x57mm caliber, although reservists sometimes carried the obsolete caliber 8x57J *Kommissiongewehr* M1888 or the caliber 11.15x60 Mauser *Infantriegewehr* M1871 & M1871/84. Some infantry companies also had a machine-gun platoon armed with three

---

15   Oelhafen, Anlage 1.

Schutztruppe soldier standing behind parapet walls – 1915. (© Namibian National Archives)

Pre-war photograph of *Schutztruppe* Officer Lieutenant Heise armed with Mauser rifle and probable 1908 Luger pistol. (© Author's Collection)

Schutztruppe Maxim Machine-gun Detachment in the field. The soldier lying directly behind the gun carries a *Kommissions Gewehr* 88 rifle. (© Namibian National Archives)

Schutztruppe mountain gun 7.5 cm L/14 M. 08 in action against native guerrillas prior to WWI. (© Namibian National Archives)

Schutztruppe artillery crew & 7.7cm FK 96 n/A gun of 3rd
Reserve Battery. (© Namibian National Archives)

venerable 7.92mm Maxim MG08 machine-guns. The Germans disposed of a number of artillery types, including twelve very mobile 7.5cm Mountain Gun *Gebirgskanone* L/14 M.08, as well as eight 7.7cm Field Canon FK 96 n/A, and twenty-two 7.7cm Field Canon FK 96 a/A.[16] At least two Krupp 37mm "Pom-pom" automatic canon and four antiquated Model 98 howitzers were deployed with formations but did not fire a round during the war. A large number of even older field guns remained in the artillery depots.

Similar to the South African UDF, the *Schutztruppe* was neither organized nor trained for combat on a large scale against a European opponent. Its experience was in fighting bush wars against small bands of indigenous soldiers and, while the Germans were fairly adept at this, few of its senior officers had the experience to lead large, combined operations. The Germans also suffered from a dearth of well-trained or experienced non-commissioned officers; many of the *Schutztruppe* veterans called up for duty had not participated in operations or even military exercises in several years.

With the declaration of war, Boers resident in GSWA volunteered to fight with the German-organized South African Free Corps (*Südafrikanischen Freiwilligen-Korps* or *Vrijkorps* in Afrikaans). The Free Corps was a single, company-sized element, supplied and equipped by the Germans and supported with one artillery battery (four FK 96 a/A canon and two Krupp automatic cannon) that was initially manned by *Schutztruppe* troopers under Captain Haußding. It was intended to augment the Boer revolt and fought several independent actions against UDF forces inside South Africa. With the failure of the Boer rebel revolt, the Free Corps was disbanded in early 1915.[17]

---

16   Although the German 7.7cm FK 96 guns were designated n/A for *neuer Art* (new model) or a/A for *alter Art* (old model) both guns were considered obsolete and most were "shot out" by the beginning of World War I.

17   The German gun crews were withdrawn and the guns turned over to the rebel Free Corps in December

Flying Lieutenant von Scheele with his Aviatik aircraft near Stingbank
– March/April 1915. (© Scientific Society Swakopmund)

Unlike Germany's other colonies, the *Schutztruppe* in GSWA did not rely heavily on indigenous soldiers because of a constant fear of native uprisings. When they were used, it was sparingly and overwhelmingly in support roles, such as drivers of supply wagons or manual laborers. Only trusted tribes were armed, such as the so-called "Rehoboth Basters" who provided one company of armed troops and were responsible for security in their semi-autonomous "Bastardland". Another, the *Kamerun Kompagnie* – a company of soldiers from Cameroon (along with many seamen from the Kru tribe of Liberia) – served in GSWA, but was disbanded during the war and only employed in manual labor or as police auxiliaries.

The Germans were also burdened by the very large logistical requirements entailed in the feeding and watering of hundreds of horses and beasts of burden. A six-gun artillery battery, for example, required a minimum of 44 mules or oxen to pull the guns, and limbers. Another 36 animals were required to pull the ammunition and equipment wagons. Water and fodder requirements aside, this was a very slow mode of transport. Unlike the South Africans who had hundreds of vehicles available, the Germans had only five automobiles in the territory.

Airplanes made an early appearance in GSWA with the arrival during the summer of 1914 of three pilots to form a new air force. Lieutenant Alexander von Scheele, along with Aviatik factory pilot Willy Trück, and Austrian reserve officer Lieutenant Paul Fiedler had two biplanes between them, an Aviatik B1 and a LFG Roland.[18] Neither airplane was suitable for the hot, desert climate of the territory but they were pressed into service

---

1914. Gordon McGregor, *Das Burenfreikorps von Deutsch-Südwestafrika, 1914-1915*, p.60.

18   Karl D Seifert, *Flieger über den Kolonien*, p.54. A third airplane, a Pfalz pusher, visited GSWA, but was transported to German East Africa just prior to hostilities where it was put to use against the British.

German civilian pilot Willi Truck and his Aviatik on arrival in
GSWA – 1914. Senior Lieutenant von Scheele took over flying duties
from Truck after the war began. (© Namibian National Archives)

nevertheless. Von Scheele piloted Aviatik in the north, while Fiedler flew the Roland in the
south. Both pilots flew many sorties over South African lines during the campaign, gaining
intelligence on the South African troop movements and occasionally dropping home made
bombs. Fiedler also managed to take photographs during his flights, which are probably the
only aerial images of the war in the territory. The last mission was flown in May 1915; both
planes were burned to prevent them from falling into enemy hands.

3

Before the Battle

Intelligence Preparations for War

A discussion of the origins of World War I would be too ambitious for this short work and to say that in the early 20th Century Britain and Germany came to regard each other as adversaries simplifies a very nuanced debate, but must suffice for our purposes.

In the late 19th Century, Britain considered France and Russia as its principal adversaries, but Kaiser Wilhelm II's bellicose rhetoric and aggressive foreign policies, including a plan to build her navy caused Britain to reconsider. Germany, without the genius of Bismarck to chart a rational course of balanced power, vacillated in its choice of allies and enemies, antagonizing one and then another. At the same time the Imperial government in Berlin naively chose to believe its colonies would not be drawn into the conflict because of its reading of the 1885 Treaty of Berlin. Britain's leaders, on the other hand, would show that they had few reservations about extending the war beyond the European theater, especially as they viewed German colonialism as a strategic threat to its Empire and commerce. In point of fact, the first shot of World War I on land was fired by a British soldier by a colonial sergeant in Togo and the last German commander to surrender would be Colonel Paul von Lettow-Vorbeck, whose forces laid down their arms in East Africa almost two weeks after the 11 November 1918 armistice in Europe.

In the early 1900s, Europe was inching towards war. Beyond the ivory towers and mirror-lined halls of power, the military leaders of Britain and Germany recognized that war was most likely inevitable and wanted to know their future opponents intentions and capabilities. In the absence of a declared war, there were a number of methodologies used by both the Germans and British to collect intelligence. Seemingly, however, the British were more accomplished at the task than their continental rivals. The South African Union Defense Force (UDF), only created in 1912, had little in the way of a functioning defense staff or intelligence organization before the war. Much of what its army required to function would be made up, cobbled together on an ad hoc basis after the leadership in Pretoria made its decision to go to war. It would have to catch up when the time for battle came.

Prior to World War I, military intelligence was a primitive art form and those who practiced it were often unappreciated by the officers and men of the line. Generally, the work was considered to be unsuitable for professional officers and those in that field were considered incapable of commanding combat troops. To complicate matters further, intelligence work generally was done on an ad hoc basis; units were formed and officers assigned as the need arose and then dispensed of when no longer needed. Although a formal military intelligence structure was created within the British Army in 1899, its field elements were disbanded in 1901, only to be recreated in 1912.[1] Even then, few enlightened

---

1   Anthony Clayton, *Forearmed: A History of the Intelligence Corps*, 10; and Thomas G Fergusson, *British Military Intelligence: 1870-1914*, pp.15, 30-31.

senior officers understood the immense value of military intelligence. During World War I, the UDF remained dependent on Britain for its requirements, as it had no organic intelligence service, only a General Staff officer with intelligence responsibilities.[2]

Methodologies

A distinction needs to be made between two general forms of military intelligence: strategic and tactical. Strategic intelligence collection is geared to obtaining information that permits one nation to understand the capabilities and intentions of another national state or entity. At the military level, it is the collection and assessment of information that will shed light on an opponent's grand strategy. This intelligence helps the commander devise a strategy to defeat the enemy. Tactical intelligence is simply the information required for planning and conducting tactical operations.

There were several methods of intelligence collection. The first and safest method of collection was the study of open source materials, ie newspapers and magazines.[3] Especially valuable were journal articles or books written by military officers that described new tactics and trends.

Military attachés assigned to embassies in foreign capitals had the ability (some more competently than others) to elicit useful information from host-country officers through discussions or from direct observation of maneuvers.[4] With the exception of the period of 1904-1908 during the Herero and Namaqua (Nama) rebellions, the British had no military representation in GSWA (the contributions of the attachés that served during that period will be discussed later).

Diplomatic reporting about parliamentary debates, as well as that of business travelers was also an important source of information. John Cleverley, for example, who was the British Resident Magistrate in Walvis Bay, ran an extensive network of informants operating in the western and central parts of the German colony and his reports were relayed to the Ministry of Defense and the Colonial Office.[5]

Cooperation with allied nations sometimes yielded good information, but the acquisition of such intelligence always had to be assessed to determine if the information was meant to influence as well as inform. Also, understanding any faulty assumptions that might have been applied to their assessment was of equal importance.

The most difficult and dangerous method was espionage by men and women on the ground – what is now called human intelligence or HUMINT. The risks entailed sometimes brought great reward, but failure could lead to a diplomatic incident or the death of an agent or asset.

Wireless intercepts as a nascent form of signals intelligence (SIGINT) also played a role

---

2   Ian Van der Waag, "The battle of Sandfontein, 26 September 1914: South African military, reform and the German South-West Africa campaign, 1914–1915", *First World War Studies, DOI: 10.1080/19475020.2013.828633*.

3   It was, and still is today, a very productive way to gain information, accounting for nearly 90 percent of overall collection. See comments by Admiral William Studeman at the First International Symposium on Open Source Solutions in December 1992, available at https://www.fas.org/irp/fbis/studem.html.

4   Military Attachés as diplomats, however, are generally forbidden from conducting *clandestine* intelligence collection.

5   Cleverley's reporting covered a wide range of topics; those on Native Affairs in the German protectorate are very negative of the German administration. Many are contained in the files at Kew especially *TNA: PRO 244.*

in the campaign. Listening to the enemy's communications, especially when radio security was poor, provided the commanders with a wealth of information on enemy dispositions and intentions.

Once the battle was joined, scouts and aerial observers were responsible for the collection of tactical information on the battlefield for the military commander to plan his operations.[6] A few examples from across the spectrum of intelligence collection will illustrate the methods used by the protagonists in this theatre of war.

On their own – the Colonial Germans

The commander of the territorial protection forces in German South West Africa had no illusions as to his precarious position, despite Berlin's naiveté. As early as 1908, he was writing classified telegrams from Windhoek to the German legations and embassies in Cape Town, Luanda, Lisbon, and London seeking information on the Portuguese troops in Angola and the British in the Cape Colony. He tasked the offices to provide him with information on the Order of Battle (OB), including on types of formations, locations, weapons, and the strength of units – with numbers of white and coloured troops. Additionally, the newest maps of Angola and the Cape Colony were requested with the promise of reimbursement.

The responses received in Windhoek often left much to be desired, as the reply from the German General Consul HP von Humboldt in Cape Town demonstrated. He declared it would be easier to ask the British in London for the information, as local inquiries might lead to mistrust. Clearly Humboldt was not a man to undertake intelligence missions for the military. The German Consul at Boma in the Belgian Congo who had responsibility for Portuguese Angola was more forthcoming and in a cable response detailed how he was able to obtain and send the latest maps and OB by courier to Windhoek. Eventually, a comprehensive outline of the military organization of the South African military was delivered, but it would be outdated by the time war began.[7]

Among the German missionaries working among the native peoples in South Africa, many retained strong ties to their homeland. Although most were suspected of spying for Berlin, many did provide information on the situation in South Africa to their society offices in Germany. Often, the true value of missionaries lay in countering misinformation and rumour. Many did provide information and, prior to World War I, their reports usually concerned the mood of the indigenous people; information that was important to Protectorate administrators concerned with cross border influences on their "own" native populations.

Several German officers travelled into the Cape Colony and reported their observations when they returned to their home base. One archive report submitted by *Schutztruppe* Senior Lieutenant Wittmann in 1909, included newspaper clippings concerning the Union Army, as well as finely detailed sketches he made of defensive points on the Cape Peninsula and the Durban Harbour Batteries. It is unknown how many such trips were undertaken, but the type of intelligence collected, especially on harbour defenses, clearly shows it may have been intended for offensive operations.[8]

---

6   Today scouts are part of what is called intelligence, reconnaissance and surveillance (ISR) forces, which form a total package of intelligence resources available to the combat commander.

7   *Geheimakten: Kommandeur – ST Mobilmachungvorarbeiten*, [Secret Files: Commander – Preparations for Mobilization of the Protection Force], ZBU 2372, IX.h.

8   Ibid.

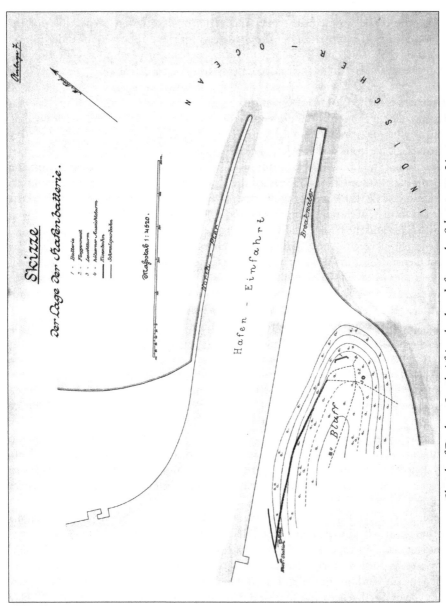

Sketch of Durban, South Africa, harbor defenses by *Schutztruppe* Lieutenant
Wittmann, 1908. (© Namibian National Archives

In 1914, despite not having a dedicated intelligence arm within the *Schutztruppe*, the Germans had a relatively clear understanding of their opponents' military structures, but little idea of their strategies. For that matter, the South Africans had no idea what their own strategy would be until war broke out.

Attachés and Spies – Britain and the German Threat

Although Britain played an ancillary role in the campaign to capture GSWA, its intelligence operations prior to the war assisted the Union's effort in specific areas.

In the late 19th and early 20th Centuries, protection of her Imperial domain was always of the utmost concern for Britain and many politicians and military officers saw the German colonization of Africa as a possible threat from its outset.

In most British colonies, colonial administrators such as magistrates were often drawn from a cadre of trained military police officers. This held true for the Cape Colony's magistrates in Bechuanaland and Walvis Bay whose job often focused on monitoring the indigenous peoples and their grievances as well as aspirations. Prior to World War I, the resident magistrates reported on native affairs in neighbouring GSWA and became familiar with the political and military situation in the German protectorate. Although colonial intelligence gathering had been given a home in the Home Section of the Secret Service Bureau created in 1909, the emphasis of that Bureau was on the threat of Bolshevism and anti-colonial movements in Britain's territories. Britain's concerns about her own colonies' indigenous populations was a major reason why she would not consider arming rebels during the 1904-1908 uprisings or later during World War I.[9] As we shall see, the South Africans may not have had that concern.

Military attachés assigned overseas were important sources of strategic intelligence information before the war and did much to inform the thinking of the British Foreign and War Offices about German intentions, as well as capabilities. British military attachés provided intelligence that was very much responsible for shaping perceptions towards Germany in the lead up to the war.

Lieutenant Colonel Frederick Trench was the British Military Attaché to the German Headquarters in GSWA from 1905 to 1906 during the Herero and Nama uprisings and in Berlin thereafter. We know little of Trench except that he was an artillery officer and veteran of the 2nd Anglo-Boer War where he earned the Distinguished Service Order. He later met Kaiser Wilhelm II, whom he apparently impressed with his German language ability and his suitability for life at court; what the Germans called *Hoffähigkeit*. The Kaiser requested Trench by name to serve as a military observer in GSWA where a ruthlessly effective commander, Lieutenant General Adrian Dietrich Lothar von Trotha, was suppressing a native rebellion. Trench's secret field reports were sent to his military superiors and to the Governor of the Cape Colony who forwarded them to the Foreign Office in London and the British Embassy in Berlin. For a little over a year Trench submitted his observations on von Trotha, the insurgency, the *Schutztruppe*, and German intentions towards the Cape Colony. A great deal of his reporting can be found in the British Army intelligence handbook *Military Report on German South-West Africa*, that was first printed in 1906 and re-issued in 1913. From archival records it is clear that much of the handbook was taken

---

9   *Letters from Resident Magistrate, Mafeking to the High Commissioner, Johannesburg*, RC 11-1: *Herero*. The British, however, had no qualms with arming colonial units like the King's African Rifles under white leadership in its own colonies.

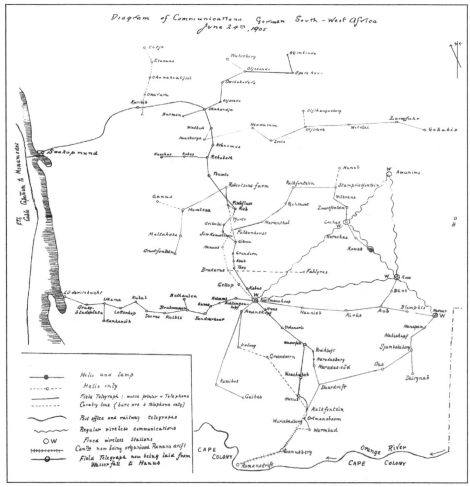

Map of German communications network obtained by British Colonel Trench
while serving as Military Attaché and observer in GSWA during the Herero
and Namaqua uprisings – 1905-06. (© Botswana National Archives)

verbatim from Trench's reports and those of his successor, Major Wade.

Trench also submitted a number of maps that that would have been valuable to
a military planner, including details of the German communications network in the
protectorate, showing rail, telegraph, and heliograph connections throughout the country.

Notably, Trench pinpointed suitable targets for destruction in the event of war, which
included the submarine telegraph cable, the wharves and piers at Swakopmund, and the
water desalinization condensers at Lüderitzbucht. With the exception of the condensers, all
of these sites were disabled or attacked in August and September 1914.[10]

---

10   The high-powered Telefunken radio transmitter and huge antennae at Windhoek and the smaller stations
at Lüderitzbucht and Swakopmund had not yet been built during Trench's time in GSWA. The British
did shell the German water condensers at Cape Cross, while those at Lüderitzbucht were saved for the
water requirements of the UDF.

In a strategic context, Trench assessed that the Germans were preparing for possible offensive action against the Cape Colony. This was a theme that Trench would continue following his reassignment to Berlin in 1906 where he reported extensively on the bellicose nature of the Germans towards England. In one report, Trench states:

> I cannot escape the impression that the suppression of the native revolt is going hand in hand with preparations for the subsequent use of the protectorate troops – or a portion of them – across the Orange River should the occasion demand it ...

The archived copy of this report is bound together with a number of translated and deciphered secret telegrams detailing logistical issues between the German Headquarters in GSWA and the German Consulate in Cape Town. Trench does not say where he obtained the telegrams, but he uses them well to illustrate his assessments. England's military attachés shaped strategic thinking prior to World War I, especially its perception of Germany as an aggressor and it is seems clear that Trench and Wade were influential in London's decisions about Germany and its colonies at the outset of the war.[11]

Few accounts of espionage in GSWA exist and fewer still are any official records of intelligence reporting. One notable exception is that of Alexander Paterson Scotland who arrived in Cape Town from Scotland in 1902. Too late to take part in the Boer War, he stayed in the colony and found work on the border between Cape Colony and GSWA, where he became involved in the ongoing rebellion, primarily supplying the German forces. According to his biography, written after World War II, he learned to speak German and actually joined the *Schutztruppe* taking part in several operations around 1905-6. All the while, he was reporting on German activities to British agents. By the time World War I rolled around, Scotland fell afoul of German authorities and was detained in Windhoek until the South Africans captured the city in July 1915. After his release he made his way to England where he continued his work in Europe as a British Army intelligence officer.[12] While spy stories are often sensational, their actual contributions are generally not so spectacular and rarely useful once the messy business of battlefield operations begins.

Late to the Game – The South Africans

At the outset of the war, the Union Defense Force was not well organized to conduct strategic intelligence operations against the Germans. The UDF's organization for meeting intelligence requirements was mostly ad hoc at the beginning and was largely focused on tactical intelligence. The General Staff section of the UDF was tasked for the mission just prior to the hastily organized invasion of GSWA and its efforts would revolve around the deployment of scouts and the newly developed art of radio intercept.

The mission of Major Langbaard Grobler is a case in point. He and his 50-man unit, known as "Grobler's Scouts", were deployed to Walvis Bay where he was instructed to collect information on the German town of Swakopmund and the surrounding area. Botha and the other Union commanders were very familiar with the employment of mounted reconnaissance scouts, having used them extensively in the Anglo-Boer War.

---

11   Frederick Trench, "War Office Papers: Despatches of Col F J A Trench", TNA: WO 186, and Matthew Seligmann, "A View From Berlin: Colonel Frederick Trench and the Development of British Perceptions of German Aggressive Intent, 1906–1910," *The Journal of Strategic Studies*, pp.114-147.
12   LTC Alexander P Scotland, *The London Cage*.

South African UDF radio intercept team. (© Namibian National Archives)

Of the importance of scouts and their product (tactical intelligence) Sir Robert Baden-Powell said:

> It has been said that "there is scarcely a battle in history which has not been won or lost in proportion to the value of the last reconnaissance." Either the winners have won through knowing all about the numbers and position of their adversaries, and have thus been able to direct their moves so as to ensure success; or the loser, through ignorance of these points, has been unable to save himself.[13]

The Germans had great respect for the Boer commandos and their scouts' capabilities. Their official history of the campaign refers to specific *Burgher* officers known for their reconnaissance skills. The history makes it clear that the South Africans also used indigenous troops to scout out the land. On 22 February 1915, a *Schutztruppe* patrol encountered and routed a South African scout element near the village of Garub, near Aus, where the Germans were facing General Mackenzie's troops. The element was made up of Namaqua natives led by a white officer; in the skirmish the officer and two Nama were killed. Upon investigation, the Germans found the dead white officer was Captain C.K. de Meillon of the Imperial Light Horse, who was in the advance guard that first landed at Lüderitzbucht. Before the war, he had lived in that town, ostensibly as a photographer

---

13   LTG Sir Robert Baden-Powell, *Aids to Scouting*, p.6. Baden-Powell, who was the creator of the Boy Scout movement in 1909, tried to inculcate the methodologies of scouts and reconnaissance duties into the British Army's cavalry training, but he was rebuffed by more senior general officers like Douglas Haig and Sir John French who felt that mounted horse troops were best suited for direct assaults with pennants and lances. The results in the European theater of war bear witness to the fallacy of their beliefs.

Native despatch runner and UDF soldier. The South Africans employed
indigenous peoples to a far greater extent than the Germans in scouting
and communications duties. (© Namibian National Archives)

and diamond prospector. These activities would have provided him excellent access to the countryside and a way to unobtrusively collect information. The Germans were sure that de Meillon must have been a spy before the war. It is equally possible he volunteered for service in the UDF and was employed in a position where his skills could be best used – as a reconnaissance scout leader.

In the Swakop River Valley campaign, Botha would employ six mounted scout elements known as "Intelligence Units", each comprised of 25 to 50 men, to carry out forward area reconnaissance in force. Botha would also make use of radio intercept operations to collect information on an enemy that employed poor communications security. The Germans had a habit of mixing encrypted traffic, usually code words or names, with "clear" or unencrypted traffic, which facilitated the South African listener's chances of breaking the codes. The Germans were somehow able to recover a South African radio intercept team's notebook from Swakopmund that contained detailed information about German operations, movements, and strengths. Strangely, that did not deter the Germans from continuing their bad habits.[14]

Knowledge of the terrain is as important as knowing the enemy and although scouts can be of great utility in this regard, good maps are better still. A recent study suggested that the South Africans did not have access to good maps of the protectorate and the

---

14   Richard Hennig, *Deutsch-Südwest im Weltkrieg*, p.121.

British produced the few that were available.[15] In fact, the official South African history of the campaign refers to "Map S.1" used by General Botha to plan the Swakop campaign. A surviving copy of this map was recently evaluated and according to the map's margin data, it is clear that it was only one of a number produced by the UDF General Staff Intelligence Topographic Section in 1915.[16] Moreover, not only was the S.1 map based on German maps from 1910 (perhaps obtained by South African traders or miners for the government) it was very accurate and comparable to modern maps. South African forces in GSWA had the luxury of good maps (albeit in extremely limited quantities), local guides, and mounted scouts all of which contributed enormously to the success of the campaign. Throughout the course of the campaign, the indigenous natives saw the South Africans as liberators – at least initially – and provided information and assistance to help rid their homeland of the German colonial oppressor. Contemporary German accounts and the official history repeatedly noted the problem of indigenous spies in their midst and attribute the failure of most booby-traps and mines to their compromise by locals who pointed them out to UDF troops as soon as the Germans departed an area.[17]

With the advent of war, tactical intelligence was to be of paramount importance and the side that possessed the best, most up to date information on his enemy and terrain would have an edge over his opponent. While the Germans had the "home field" advantage, they would rapidly lose it to the South Africans who made better and more aggressive use of intelligence methodologies.

---

15   Lt Col André Jacobs, and Cdr Hennie Smit, "Topographic Mapping Support In The South African Military During The 20th Century", *Scientia Militaria*, pp.32-50.

16   According to Collyer, the UDF's Topographic Section was one of the few intelligence elements capable of providing support to the field forces, and then only to the Northern Force and with limited capabilities; it had four men and one wagon during the campaign.

17   Hans von Oelhafen, *Der Feldzug in Südwest 1914-1915*, pp.155, 209, 222.

4

Battle Plans

The Political Objectives of Britain and South Africa

The German presence in South West Africa (GSWA) had been an irritant to the United Kingdom and its dominion, the Union of South Africa, since Reichschancellor Bismarck declared the territory to be a German protectorate in 1884. While Bismarck's move was intended primarily to protect German trade and business in foreign areas not already claimed by other countries, Britain regarded Germany's role as a colonial power with mixed feelings. On one hand, it felt Germany could share in the responsibility of civilizing Africa. On the other, Germany was seen as a leader in a global "anti-British conspiracy," especially at the turn of the century.

Prior to 1884, the United Kingdom was interested only in its port enclave at Walvis Bay and the nearby coastal islands that were important sources of guano for the Cape Colony. Britain rebuffed the Cape Government's request that it annex the territory surrounding the enclave as it saw no commercial potential in the area and did not wish to expand further its territorial holdings in the region. It was only on Germany's entry into the colonial rush for Africa that Britain became concerned with the German presence near its own colonies and shipping lanes.

Once Britain began to perceive Germany as a threat, the protectorate of GSWA and the other German possessions of Togo, Cameroon, and East Africa, as well as those in the Pacific, were seen to endanger the Royal Navy and its maritime foreign commerce.[1] Even prior to World War I, the British Admiralty was extremely concerned with the activities and striking power of Admiral Graf Maximilian von Spee's East Asian Squadron that was roaming the southern seas. David Lloyd George would later write that one of Britain's basic war aims in 1914 was nothing less than the "destruction of the German colonial system" to ensure the future security of Britain communications and its Imperial position in Africa.[2]

South African leader Prime Minister Louis Botha had long felt that South West Africa would be better served if annexed to the Union and, as early as 1911 and again in 1913, expressed to Winston Churchill his intent to "attack German South West Africa and clear them (the Germans) all out once and for all."[3] Like Rhodes before them, Botha and Smuts harbored the dream of incorporating Rhodesia, Bechuanaland and Nyasaland into the Union.[4] The conquest of South West Africa would contribute to their aspiration of uniting the whole of southern Africa under the Union flag.[5]

---

1   Shawn T. Grimes, *Strategy and War Planning in the British Navy, 1887-1918*, p.71 and Matthew Seligmann, *The Royal Navy and the German Threat 1901-1914: Admiralty Plans to Protect British Trade in a War Against Germany*, pp.10-12.

2   David Lloyd George, *War Memoirs*, p.910.

3   Winston S. Churchill, *My Early Life*: 1874-1904, p.255.

4   Bechuanaland and Nyasaland are the modern countries of Botswana and Malawi.

5   In 1918, Botha would write to Smuts in London imploring him to consider an "exchange" with Portugal to trade the conquered area of German East Africa for Portugal's port at Lourenco Marques in Delagoa Bay, part of Mozambique, in order to further expand South Africa's territory. Martin Chanock,

At the beginning of World War I, His Majesty's Government in London recognized that the conquest of GSWA and the other German colonies would eliminate an immediate security threat to the Royal Navy. Some South African leaders thought the Union would reap other benefits such as safeguarding the dominion of South Africa and promoting a better relationship with England. General Jan Smuts, Botha's Minister of Defense, was also convinced that such a campaign would provide a means to promote internal unity between South Africa's English and Boer populations. Author Hew Strachan, stated in his book *The First World War in Africa,* that across Europe, there was a feeling that the war would replace "domestic discord by renewed national purpose, a sense of union that conquered class and ethnic divisions."[6] This was not the case in South Africa where the South African leadership underestimated the level of enmity felt by the Boer against England that would lead to an internal revolt. While the revolt would be short lived, it did disrupt South African plans for a quick conquest.

Botha was the prime mover in South Africa's strategic thinking. It was he who, early in August 1914, recommended that Britain remove its troops from South Africa, thereby freeing them to be deployed in Europe, and offered to conduct the self-defense of South Africa with UDF troops alone. London gratefully accepted Botha's offer, but responded with a new request that South Africa take on an "urgent Imperial service." This service was to capture the massive German radio station at Windhoek, while also seizing the two ports towns of Swakopmund and Lüderitzbucht. It was a mission similar to expeditions the British would undertake against the German colonies in West and East Africa to eliminate the German Imperial Navy's communications links and deny its commercial fleet any safe-haven. Botha was only too happy to comply, as this would provide him the opportunity to gain control of South West Africa once and for all.

Botha used two small border incidents that took place, one at Nakob on 10 August 1914, the other at Liebenberg, on the northern frontier of South Africa in late August to convince his wavering cabinet and parliament to go to war – a decision that he had already made and for which the plans and mobilization were already under way. The "propagandization" of these two events, labeled "invasions" by the press – in one case little more than a failed German attempt to stop resident Boer farmers taking their cattle out of the territory to the Cape Colony and the other an apparent map reading error on a vaguely defined border – was crucial to convincing the public at large that an imminent German invasion presented a clear danger to South Africa and that war was necessary. Colonel J.J. Collyer, Chief of Staff for the UDF, later stated it was known at the time that the incursions were not indicative of a German intention to invade.[7] Nevertheless, the South African war machine was put into gear for action.

The South African Battle Plan

It was Smuts and his senior officers, among them Brigadier Generals C.F. Beyers, H.T. "Tim" Lukin, Duncan McKenzie, and Colonels P.S. Beves and P.C.B. Skinner, who made the plans for the initial invasion that took place in September 1914. Smuts knew that the UDF possessed overwhelming power compared to the German *Schutztruppen*, which he believed could not muster more than 5,000 active, reserve, and *Landwehr/Landsturm*

Unconsummated Union: Britain, Rhodesia and South Africa, 1900-45, p.114.

6   Hew Strachan, *The First World War in Africa*, p.60.

7   Collyer, p.22.

South African troops landing at Lüderitzbucht. (© Namibian National Archives)

(Home Defense) officers and men. Smuts initially wanted to simultaneously land troops at Lüderitzbucht in the south and at Swakopmund, GSWA's principal seaport and the direct route to the central part of the territory and its capital, Windhoek. This plan was hampered by a lack of transport and coordination with the Royal Navy, coupled with a fear of Admiral Tirpitz's East Asian Squadron sailing somewhere near South America. Instead it was decided to make a single landing at Lüderitzbucht.[8] Additional forces located at Port Nolloth and Upington were to conduct an invasion across the Orange River (South Africa's northern border) and from the southeast through Bechuanaland across the Kalahari Desert into GSWA. This would be followed by a drive along the central railway that ran from Keetmanshoop through the capital of Windhoek to Tsumeb in the far north of the colony.

The landing at Lüderitzbucht was a compromise, and while control of this port would deliver the southwestern part of the territory to Smuts, it provided only limited access to the north of the colony as the Namib Desert restricted movement. In any event, this plan would be undone by internal discontent resulting from Botha's decision to go to war and the German ambush of Lukin's forces at Sandfontein.

Many Boers disagreed with what they called "Britain's war" against Germany, which had supported the Boer Republics during their two wars of independence. With memories of British "barbarism" still fresh in his mind, General C.F. Beyers, the commandant general of the UDF and a fellow Boer like Botha and Smuts, was opposed to an invasion of GSWA. Other officers like General J.H. "Koos" de la Rey and Solomon G. Maritz were sympathetic to Beyers. The most influential of these, de la Rey would be accidentally killed at a police roadblock, but Maritz and others (Generals Beyers, Andries De Wet, and J.C.G. Kemp) would soon resign and rebel against the Government.

---

8   Strachan, pp.66-69.

Smuts' initial invasion plan met with disaster with the defeat of a strong advance element of General Lukin's "A Force" on September 26, 1914 at Sandfontein. That, coupled with an open revolt by Boer army officers and troops in the northern provinces of the Free State and Transvaal, forced Botha to halt his offensive against GSWA and focus on regaining control of South Africa. It would be nearly five months before the Union forces could resume offensive operations against the Germans. When they did, Botha's plan would be straightforward: an asymmetric offensive in which an overwhelmingly large force would drive into GSWA slowly and deliberately rolling up the small German force that it faced.

When the offensive did resume, General Botha would personally lead the South Africans into the heart of Germany's colony.

German Plans

At the outbreak of the First World War, GSWA's governor and commander of the *Schutztruppe* believed they had few options. Earlier in the century, Chief of the German Greater General Staff Helmut von Moltke contemplated an invasion of the Cape Colony in the case of war in Europe. He opined the protectorate would be quickly cut off and invading South Africa would be the only option open to the protectorate before her supplies ran out. Moltke and his staff also hoped that Cape Colony's Boer population would join with Germany to fight against England. Despite Moltke's plans, by 1914 the Germans were fully aware the time had passed for any such offensive enterprise.[9]

Germany was a relative latecomer and sometimes-reluctant player in the colonial game. The high costs required to maintain its expensive protectorates in Africa and the Pacific often led to conflict between the Emperor and parliament, the *Reichstag*, in Berlin. GSWA was not excluded from this debate and, following the 1904-1908 Herero and Namaqua rebellions, the *Schutztruppe* force was drastically reduced to save money.

The ordered reduction of military manpower from over 14,000 to less than 2,000 after 1912 made Moltke's recommended course of action unrealistic. The *Schutztruppe* had neither the manpower to sustain an attack nor the transport to move troops and maintain a logistical lifeline that would extend beyond the colony's southern border. An inopportune landing of enemy forces at Lüderitzbucht would also subject a German invasion force to possible encirclement and destruction. With these critical shortcomings in mind, Lieutenant Colonel Joachim von Heydebreck explored the feasible courses of action for defending the protectorate with Governor Theodor von Seitz.

As a result of his meetings, von Seitz, as the Kaiser's senior official of the protectorate, issued his directive for its defense on August 6, 1914 to Heydebreck who would be responsible for its implementation and, importantly, was in full agreement with its salient points. The *Schutztruppe* would not be employed in rash attacks on a numerically and materially superior enemy force; it would leave the offensive initiative to the South Africans. Both men saw the purpose of the *Schutztruppe* as a delaying force; to draw in the Union forces and to offer sustained resistance that would fix them militarily and economically in the territory for as long as possible so they could not be used elsewhere.[10] If Germany won the war as expected, then life in the colony could return to normal. If not, the colony would be lost anyway.

---

9   Kriegsgeschichtliche Forschungsanstalt des Heeres (KFH), *Der Feldzug in Deutsche Südwestafrika, 1914-1915,* p.16.

10   Hans von Oelhafen, *Der Feldzug in Südwest 1914-1915,* p.13.

When von Seitz issued the order for mobilization (*Mobilmachung*) he outlined the *Schutztruppe's* mission as follows:

1) Secure the protectorate against the "external enemy, increase border security, and attack only in response to enemy actions."
2) Secure the territory against indigenous and non-German elements. Politically questionable persons, either indigenous or non-Germans (eg Europeans), are to be arrested.
3) Resume connections with parties in South Africa hostile to England.[11]

Von Seitz assessed that an attack against the Union would serve no purpose politically and would sway South African (read Boer) opinion against Germany. In fact, the Germans had been in loose contact with a number of pro-German Boers since at least 1910, including South African Lieutenant Colonel S.F. "Mannie" Maritz, who would ultimately lead a short-lived rebellion against his Government in late 1914. Maritz specifically requested the Germans not attack Union territory. For these reasons, von Seitz instructed Heydebreck to avoid attacks over the border at all costs, but also to resist any South African offensives into GSWA. Von Seitz's intent to contact anti-British parties was clearly meant to encourage a rebellion against the South African government and fell in line with the German Greater General Staff's earlier assessment that the Boers would act essentially as a surrogate force for Germany. Both he and Heydebreck felt that a successful defense of the protectorate would rely heavily on a Boer uprising. The *Schutztruppe* commander immediately put into motion the measures necessary to fulfill von Seitz's orders. Defense of the southern border was his primary concern as this was where the first South African offensive was (correctly) expected. Heydebreck would concentrate his attention on the line of communications along the railway from Lüderitzbucht to Keetmanshoop and on the southern border between Ramansdrift and GSWA's eastern border. He assumed the terrain and the desire to gain control of the territory's north-south railway would channel South African movements into these areas. This was where the Germans would focus their attention.

Heydebreck discounted an attack from Angola in the north. While he assessed the Portuguese to be hostile, they had little capability or desire for offensive action against Germany. The eastern border was believed to be an effective barrier to an attack as the Kalahari Desert was generally impassable with the exception of a few routes that were exceptionally difficult. A small contingent of British South African Police was present in Rhodesia, but here again Heydebreck believed they would not play a role in GSWA; he thought it more likely that they would be deployed against German East Africa.

Although the northern and eastern borders were believed relatively secure, observation of the area by small detachments was to be maintained. The Germans feared a resurgence of indigenous violence and thought it likely refugees from the 1904-1908 Herero and Namaqua (Hottentot) rebellions who had escaped into Bechuanaland might be encouraged or supported by the British to cross back into the German protectorate and resume their fight.

The western coastal area was more problematic. Lüderitzbucht and Swakopmund, the protectorate's two port cities, were its gateways and the only connections to Germany

11 Oelhafen, p.10.

Swakopmund harbor facilities and lighthouse; the radio station
antenna is shown at left. (© Namibian National Archives)

Schutztruppe engineers dynamiting the railway line, near Aus about 100 kiometers
east of Lüderitzbucht in Southern Namibia. (© Namibian National Archives)

once the land borders were closed. Further, the British enclave of Walvis Bay lay only 30 kilometers south of Swakopmund and provided an excellent harbor and landing point for an invasion force. The towns lacked prepared defenses and von Seitz and Heydebreck did not believe they had the capability to refuse a landing at any one of these points, let alone all of them, for an extended period. For this reason, they were abandoned but for small holding forces and reconnaissance elements that were posted on the outskirts. All provisions and military supplies were withdrawn from the coastal areas, brought inland, and stockpiled. Once that was accomplished, Heydebreck ordered the railway lines leading inland from Lüderitzbucht and Swakopmund dismantled.[12]

Swakopmund was declared an open city. At this stage, the German forces had approximately a one-year reserve of supplies and munitions. They were completely cut-off from Germany and any hope of resupply or receiving additional manpower was out of the question. While the population of GSWA was in an exuberant mood with the declaration of war, von Seitz and Heydebreck worried they were *auf verlorenem Posten* – fighting for a lost cause.[13]

The Opening Gambit

After several small border skirmishes provided justification for hostilities against the Germans, Prime Minister General Louis Botha gave his Minister of Defense General J.C. Smuts responsibility to plan a campaign to seize the territory. Smuts' initial plan was a simple advance that would penetrate straight into GSWA from South Africa using three elements totaling 15,000 men. One force would seize Lüderitzbucht, the protectorate's southernmost port and gateway to the lucrative diamond-mining region, while a second would drive north through the center from Ramansdrift; a third would enter GSWA across the southeastern border with British Bechuanaland. The three-prong attack could then proceed to roll up the small German force by conducting what can only be described as a classical frontal assault. These efforts, however, would fail badly with the debacle at Sandfontein.

Initially, the UDF moved slowly in its campaign against the German protectorate. On 31 August 31 1914, "Force A" under Brigadier General H. "Tim" Lukin was landed at Port Nolloth on the northwest coast of South Africa and made its way to by rail to Steinkopf where Lukin made his temporary headquarters. This element was to divert the enemy's attention from Lüderitzbucht while "Force C", led by Colonel P.S. Beves, was making a landing there. Lukin moved his forces north to the border and on 12 September 1914, a sub-element of that force under Colonel Dawson crossed the Orange River at Ramansdrift and quickly seized the German police post on the north bank, thereby opening hostilities in southern Africa. Lukin then ordered a small reconnaissance element forward to Sandfontein, a water point about 20 kilometers north of the border that was considered critical to the Union advance to Warmbad in the south-central part of the German territory. The Germans monitored their every move.[14]

Lukin followed the initial reconnaissance with a small force under Colonel Ronald C. Grant, sending them forward towards Sandfontein. By 25 September, some 300 Union

---

12 Oelhafen, pp.10-11.
13 KFH, p.18.
14 Gerald L'Ange, *Urgent Imperial Service: South African Forces in German South West Africa, 1914-1915*, p.27.

South African encampment at Tschaukaib – 1914. (© Namibian National Archives)

UDF Commandos advancing. (© Namibian National Archives)

German *Schutztruppe* Lieutenant Voigts in observation post. (© Namibian National Archives)

Schutztruppe Maxim Machine-gun detachment in position. A range-finder is in use at rear.(© Scientific Society Swakopmund (Incorporated Association – not for Gain))

Lieutenant Fiedler's photo of Tschaukaib after he dropped bombs on the UDF camp –
1914. (© Scientific Society Swakopmund (Incorporated Association – not for Gain))

mounted troops, a section of two Quick Firing 13-pounder cannon, and a machine-gun detachment were in position. It was, however, a precarious position that had been judged indefensible by earlier reconnaissance elements. The small force occupied the low-lying terrain around the wells, while hills dominated the surrounding area. Meanwhile, the remainder of Lukin's Force "A" was strung out over 100 miles to the south. This initial foray into GSWA by a small Union force was ill prepared, thinly stretched, lacked critical intelligence about the enemy, and was about to meet with disaster.

The Germans under Lieutenant Colonel Joachim von Heydebreck were ready and had prepared an ambush. Heydebreck's troops encircled Grant's force using the higher, strategic terrain and attacked from all sides. A fierce 10-hour battle ensued. Hearing of the engagement, Lukin sent reinforcements to assist Grant, but as they advanced north, they were intercepted by a German blocking force and repulsed. After a gallant struggle with losses on both sides, Colonel Grant saw the futility of further combat and was forced to surrender his remaining forces on 26 September 1914.[15]

To the west, South African Colonel Beves and his Force "C" met no resistance and occupied Lüderitzbucht in mid-September without incident. However, the Germans had made it impossible for Beves to achieve his goal of destroying the radio station as they had dismantled it before he ever reached the port and successfully re-erected it much further inland at Aus. Perhaps in frustration, the South Africans shipped the civilian populace of the town to South Africa and interned them there as POWs for the duration of the war.

Contributing to the disaster at Sandfontein were the actions of a South African officer, Lieutenant Colonel "Mannie" Maritz, the Force "B" commander who was located

---

15   Rodney C. Warwick, "The Battle of Sandfontein: The Role and Legacy of Major General Sir Henry Timson Lukin", http://www.ajol.info/index.php/smsajms/article/view/75310

Schutztruppe Machine-gun Company on patrol in the
Auasbergen – 1914. (© Namibian National Archives)

at Upington in north-central Cape Province. Maritz's forces had been ordered to support
Lukin, but he wavered, saying his troops were not ready and were ill equipped for action. In
reality, he had already planned to desert with his command of around 1,000 rifles and rebel
against his leaders in opposition to the war against Germany. Maritz had developed close
relations with the Germans long before the war and met with the German high command
to offer his services on 15 September 1914 at Ukamas in the south of GSWA. His offer was
accepted and it was agreed that Maritz would undertake his rebellion inside South Africa.
A battery of old *Feld Kanone* FK 96 a/A artillery pieces was given to the *Freikorps,* a small
unit of Boer rebels raised inside German South West Africa to support Maritz and the
other rebels. The German leadership planned that Maritz and the *Freikorps* would act as a
surrogate force; von Seitz had ordered that no German troops would cross the border and
possibly incite anti-German sentiment.[16]

Maritz betrayed South Africa and his actions would force the Union Defense Force
to halt its operations against the Germans until the revolt in South Africa was dealt with.

Commander in Chief Louis Botha then decided to personally take the war to the heart
the German territory and on 28 November 1914, he telegraphed the British Government to
announce he was ready to begin the invasion again.

---

16   The Germans made a single substantive combat foray onto South African soil during the war when
     Schutztruppe Senior Lieutenant Friedrich Freiherr von Hadeln's reconnaissance detachment attacked
     Kakamas in February 1915 to support a failed offensive by Maritz's rebels.

5

Up the River

Operations of the *Kustenschutzabteilung* in August / September 1914

Lieutenant Colonel von Heydebreck anticipated the British would land troops both at Lüderitzbucht and Walvis Bay and he tried to plan his defenses accordingly. He knew they would come, but he felt his force could not directly oppose the landings as British warships would probably escort the troop ships and the Germans had no coastal defenses to withstand their overwhelming firepower. Heydebreck opted for a defense that would initially focus on the south. A landing of forces at Walvis Bay on the central coast, while possible, was thought to be less of a probability, thus few forces were devoted to protecting that approach. When the South Africans crossed the Orange River and landed troops at Lüderitzbucht in mid-September, Heydebreck had his forces dispersed along the southern border and a blocking force was in place at Aus. The Germans believed they were in a good position to resist and delay what they thought would be the enemy's main axis of advance.[1]

Heydebreck gave Captain Schultetus command of the *Kustenschutzabteilung* (Coastal Defense Detachment), an ad hoc element whose mission was to monitor activities at Walvis Bay and Swakopmund, as well as the inland routes from the coast. His sector of operations was from the British coastal enclave to Cape Cross. Schultetus assembled a force from active soldiers, reservists, and available *Landespolizei* officers to carry out the mission. This element was reinforced with a small detachment from the 2nd Reserve Company stationed in Karibib, but with only 100 men in total, Schultetus could accomplish little offensively. For the moment, the detachment conducted mounted patrols and relied on an observation post (OP) situated high up on Langer Heinrich Mountain to monitor activities at Walvis Bay. The OP served as a heliograph signaling post for the German camp at Riet and, on a clear day, the soldiers posted there could see the port 90 kilometers to the southwest easily.[2]

Sensing that British warships soon would be patrolling the coast, the German cargo ships in port hurriedly offloaded their cargos and headed for the open sea, hoping to find sanctuary in South America. The first weeks passed without incident until a British auxiliary cruiser, the converted Union Castle Liner *Armadale Castle*, shelled Swakopmund on 14 September trying to destroy the wireless station and lighthouse. The attack failed to knock out the antennas or the tower, but did damage the customs house and a number of private homes. At one point the British Captain asked to "parley" and Schultetus was brought on board. The German commander angrily accused the British of indiscriminately destroying private property and endangering civilians. Schultetus' diatribe was punctuated with several explosions as German engineers, apparently to emphasize his point, blew up the wireless antenna to remove it as a military target.[3] With nothing more to discuss,

---

1   *Kriegsgeschichtliche Forschungsanstalt des Heeres (KFH), Der Feldzug in Deutsche Südwestafrika, 1914-1915*, p.66.

2   Dr H.J. Rust, "Aus meinem Leben", *Newsletter of the South West African Scientific Society*.

3   When the shelling started, LTC von Heydebreck was notified and he gave the order to destroy the station. The wireless station at Lüderitzbucht had, in the meantime, been dismantled and moved inland to Aus

Schutztruppe Captain Schultetus heading out from Swakopmund
to the *Armadale Castle* to discuss the shelling. (© Scientific Society
Swakopmund (Incorporated Association – not for Gain))

Schultetus returned ashore to carry on his stalwart defense of the coast.

The Germans cleared Swakopmund of everything that could be useful, including food, supplies, and equipment. Anything immovable that might be of use to the enemy was disabled and all military age males were evacuated inland. Only a few civilians remained in the town.

Thus far, Schultetus had left the British in Walvis Bay unmolested, but after the border incidents in the south and the opening of hostilities, he mounted a raid. On 24 September, he rode into the town with 17 riflemen, confronted the magistrate and demanded the enclave's weapons. The magistrate turned over 52 rifles and a machine-gun that were destroyed. Schultetus then led his party to the port where they failed to put the cargo-handling crane out of action, but succeeded in setting the docks and a berthed tug on fire.

The British answered the incursion by first firing at the patrol from the sea as it withdrew from the town and then shelling Swakopmund's pier. This time the shelling came from another auxiliary cruiser, the *Kinfauns Castle*, and its captain announced that the shelling would be repeated if the Germans attacked Walvis Bay again. The same ship would return several times in October to drop a further forty shells on the town and again in November, destroying much of the cargo handling equipment on the pier – a gesture the

beyond the reach of the Royal Navy's guns.

Shelling of Swakopmund by British auxiliary cruiser *Kinfauns Castle*, 24 September 1914. (© Scientific Society Swakopmund (Incorporated Association – not for Gain))

Schutztruppe Reiter Paul Wlotzka at the door of his house following the shelling of Swakopmund on 14 September 1914 by the *Armadale Castle*. (© Scientific Society Swakopmund (Incorporated Association – not for Gain))

Major Franke photographed prior to taking command of the *Schutztruppe*. He is wearing his *Pour le Mérite* award earned for his actions at Omaruru during the Herero Revolt of 1904-1905. (Postcard: original photographer unknown) (© Author's Collection)

Schutztruppe, 2nd Reserve Company at Riet, Lt. Mueller, Lt. Mansfeld, 1914. (© Namibian National Archives)

A *Schutztruppe* artillery unit encampment in the Swakop
River Valley. (© Namibian National Archives)

South Africans would lament when they later needed it for offloading.

Schultetus continued his patrols throughout the months of October to December. The British evacuated Walvis Bay leaving only indigenous peoples behind, which led to local banditry around the town and into the countryside. The German patrols suppressed this activity, but there was little else for the detachment to do besides monitoring the routes inland and waiting for the expected landing. For the time being, operations continued without further incident except for an occasional run-in with the British Royal Navy, which had a penchant for shelling the coastline whenever it observed a German patrol in the dunes.

Naulila and the Loss of the Commander

In October 1914, far to the north on the border with Portuguese Angola, an incident took place that would needlessly divert the Germans. A small German delegation of nine Europeans, along with a number of local police auxiliaries, servants, and drovers, led by District Commissioner Dr Schultze-Jena, was detailed to make contact with a Portuguese official to determine the state of relations between Portugal and Germany. Schultze-Jena was to determine whether or not a state of war existed between the two countries and if there was not, to see if a route for communications and logistics could be set up – one that would circumvent the need to use Lüderitzbucht or Swakopmund. The party, which included several *Schutztruppe* officers and men, reached the border near Erikson's Drift on the Kunene River on 16 October. Schultze-Jena dispatched a scouting patrol to make contact with the Portuguese. The next day, the Germans were approached by a larger armed party led by a Lieutenant Serano and asked to ride to Fort Naulila some 15 kilometers distant on the river to meet with the officer responsible for the area. The Germans, despite having doubts about the situation, rode forward the following day and were dismayed to find the man they were to meet had ostensibly just left. Schultze-Jena was furious at being led on and attempted to depart with his escort, whereupon Serano ordered his men to fire. Schultze-Jena and three *Schutztruppen* were killed instantly while three indigenous scouts were wounded; these the Portuguese threw into the river to feed the crocodiles.

News of the ambush took several days to reach Heydebreck in the far south of the protectorate, but when it did, he ordered Major Victor Franke to lead a punitive expedition. Departing Kalkfontein-Süd on 26 October, Franke took two mounted infantry companies with four Maxim MG 08 machine-guns, a four-gun mountain-artillery battery, and *Halb Batterie Weiherr*, a half-battery of 7.7cm FK 96 n/A guns.[4] They moved first by train to Otjiwarango, then overland to the border, arriving near Fort Naulila on 16 December. The fort was encircled and attacked on 18 December, the 350 Germans managing to surprise the 1,000 Portuguese defenders despite indications that they knew the Germans were coming. After roughly four hours of battle, the fort fell with a panicking mass of defenders choosing to run away. The Germans lost 11 men while the Portuguese lost nearly 200 killed and 66 captured.

In an episode telling of the state of relations between the indigenous peoples and their Lusophone colonizers, local Oshivambo villagers fell on the fleeing Portuguese and killed scores more. Discipline fell apart in the region forcing the Portuguese manning the nearby forts to retreat northwards to the safety of the coastal towns. Before returning south, Franke's expedition sought out and destroyed the remaining Portuguese military posts along the border.[5]

As it turned out, Portugal was not yet at war with Germany. Nonetheless, Lisbon dispatched an elite marine infantry regiment to the port city of Mossamedes in late December 1914 to reinforce the colony's forces, but it arrived too late to influence events at Naulila and the Portuguese would not venture south for the duration of the war. Once his mission was complete, Franke's force returned south to rejoin their comrades. The German response was justifiable, but unwise in that it diverted forces that could have been better employed against the primary threat.

In the meantime, disaster had struck the main force. On 9 November, troops at Kalkfontein-Süd test fired a new rifle grenade system. The first six shots went off without problem, but a seventh grenade exploded prematurely killing one trooper immediately and wounding four others of the team. Observing the practice, Lieutenant Colonel Heydebreck and Medical Officer Dr Berg were wounded. Over the next days, Heydebreck's condition worsened and despite surgery, he died on 12 November. Major Franke was named as his successor, but as he was on the Naulila expedition, Major Ritter took over as temporary commander.[6] With the loss of Heydebreck, the *Schutztruppe* was left without a commander who had a clear operational vision of how to defend the territory.

In December 1914, Major Ritter, who was in temporary command of the *Schutztruppe* at Aus, believed he had enough combat power to slow the South African's advance out of

---

4   Victor Franke, *Tagesbuch: 1896-1920*, p.950. While the South African commandos were usually named after the township where they were formed, German units often carried their commander's name.

5   Max Baericke, Naulila: *Errinerungen eines Zeitgenossen*, II.5b-6; Oelhafen, pp.76-92.

6   Hans von Oelhafen, *Der Feldzug in Südwest 1914-1915*, p.55.

Schutztruppe 2nd Reserve Company ready to depart, Aukas
at Khan River. (© Namibian National Archives)

Lüderitzbucht. He also thought the forces near Walvis Bay, with the addition of Franke's element, could turn back any enemy that landed there. The Germans assessed that any enemy landing at Walvis or Swakopmund would be nothing more than a demonstration of force. If necessary, Ritter felt he could delay them along the southern front and then hurriedly shift north to reinforce the *Kustenschutzabteilung* and destroy any forces attempting to move out from Walvis Bay.[7]

Ritter assigned General Staff Officer Captain Weck the task of defending the northern approaches calling this element *Kommando Rechter Flügel* (Right Wing Command). For this task, Weck had only the *Kustenschutzabteilung* reinforced by the remainder of the 2nd Reserve Company that had recently arrived at Jakalswater. Also available to him were two undermanned replacement companies at Karibib and Johann-Albrechtshöhe further inland, a machine-gun detachment in Windhoek, 250 kilometers to the east, and an artillery battery in Seeis, 300 kilometers distant. In other words, he would have no significant combat power to oppose the enemy until the arrival of *Regiment Naulila* in March.

The Germans' fragile position was eroded even further by events beyond the control of Ritter or Franke. Far away in the South Atlantic, the German East-Asian Squadron under Admiral Graf Spee was sailing off the coast of South America near the Falkland Islands. They intended to attack the Royal Navy coaling base at Port Stanley. They met a superior

---

7   KFH, 66-68.

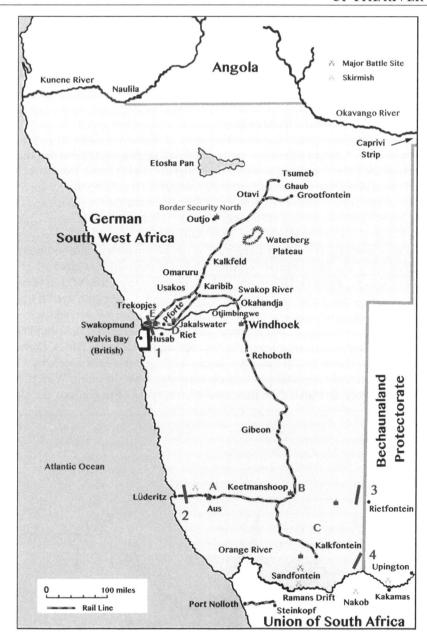

General Dispositions of German and South African allied in forces
in GSWA at the beginning of March 1915. (© James Stejskal)

British fleet under Admiral Sturdee instead and four of the squadron's warships were sunk. With the removal of the only threat to their operations along the southern coast of Africa, the British could step up support to the South Africans. This development dramatically changed the military situation in the protectorate as it effectively removed any German hope of relief from the sea.

Walvis Bay – Christmas Night, 1914

Fog and darkness obscured the British enclave port of Walvis Bay from observation as a small patrol led by Captain Schultetus approached on a reconnaissance mission the night of December 25, 1914. The patrol that December night proved different from those before. With no moon and a heavy coastal fog, visibility was near zero. As the patrol approached the town, pickets from the South African Rand Rifles detected their approach and opened fire, forcing it back into the coastal dunes for cover. Schultetus took his unit back to its camp at Dorstriviermund up the Swakop River Valley.

The next morning, the OP on Langer Heinrich Mountain was able to observe two British Navy cruisers, two auxiliary cruisers, and nine troopships in the harbor. Some 400 Union Defense Force (UDF) troops had already been offloaded. Within hours, two infantry brigades, the Imperial Light Horse (ILH), and a seven-gun artillery brigade landed unopposed on the docks of the enclave. This was Northern Force, which would be commanded by Colonel P.C.B. Skinner until the arrival of General Botha in mid-February 1915. After the Sandfontein debacle and the Boer uprising inside South Africa, Botha's new plan dispensed with the "A", "B", and "C" forces, creating instead the Southern, Central, and Eastern Forces, which would continue the campaign from the south. With these and his Northern Force at Walvis Bay, Botha would renew the offensive into the German

South African troops disembarking from a barge at the Old
Pier at Walvis Bay. (© Namibian National Archives)

protectorate.

The Germans seriously underestimated the strength of the enemy at Walvis Bay. On 2 January 1915, Captain Weck erroneously reported via radio that he faced approximately one cavalry regiment and four infantry companies. He also thought the enemy had no offensive intentions at that time.[8] By this time, Franke had returned from the north and was fully in command of all *Schutztruppe* forces. He assessed the landing at Walvis was only a demonstration of force and that the main threat still came from the enemy forces at Lüderitzbucht in the south. There, General MacKenzie was building up his forces and repairing the damaged railway for an anticipated push inland. A major camp for his 5,000-man mounted force was established at Tschaukaib, 60 kilometers inland. To supply the soldiers and their approximately 8,000 horses and mules with water, the South African Engineer Corps under Lieutenant Colonel R Francis Collins had to find and clear the few existing boreholes in the desert. When that proved insufficient, trains brought water from Lüderitzbucht; water that had been shipped in from Cape Town or condensed from seawater. The 800 Germans in front of them prepared their defensive positions in the rocky hills west of Aus and waited.

Waiting for Botha

In early January 1915, Skinner moved his force cautiously north towards Swakopmund. Before the war, Swakopmund served as the territory's seaside resort as well as the direct link to the inland capital of Windhoek. Along with Lüderitzbucht, these two towns were the protectorate's only logistical links to Germany.

On 13 January, Skinner sent Grobler's Scouts to reconnoiter the route forward and then personally led a 350-man reconnaissance in force, comprised primarily of troopers from the ILH, to occupy the town, forcibly if necessary. Skinner's element moved north along the coast under the watchful eye of a Royal Navy cruiser offshore. When he and his troops saw the town for the first time the next morning, it was quiet, having been evacuated by the Germans the previous September. It appeared to the South Africans that the occupation would take place without incident. The Germans had other ideas. Something the Germans did have in quantity was explosives and before they withdrew from an area, they emplaced mines. Simple to construct and easy to place in the deep sands along the beach, these deadly traps waited silently for the South Africans.

Skinner led his troops through the sand dunes that lined the coast to reach a final overlook south of the Swakop River. The dry river acted as a border of sorts between the enclave and the protectorate. As Skinner and his staff observed the town for activity, four mines went off at the end of the ridgeline, killing two troopers and their mounts.

The South African commander began to consolidate his hold on the coast around Walvis Bay and Swakopmund while supply dumps and camps were established to accommodate the arriving troops. The UDF contingent secured its defensive positions and turned to the east, but halted at Swakopmund's outskirts where the force remained rooted on the coast for several weeks. Botha was slowly building up his contingents both at Lüderitzbucht in the south, but more importantly at Swakopmund, which was now the primary focus of his plan.

During the lull, a cat and mouse game ensued in the dunes around Swakopmund.

---

8   Oelhafen, pp.160-161.

German sniper fire and mines harassed the 1st Rhodesian Regiment's guard posts on the eastern approach to the town as well as the South Africans when they entered the dunes on patrol.

The mines were a specialty of retired Austrian Lieutenant Venuleth, who cobbled together all the explosives and shrapnel he could find to disrupt the enemy's patrolling. Venuleth would eventually place many mines and booby traps along the German withdrawal route, many rigged to go off by the opening of a house door or gate, others by the footfall of a man or animal.[9] Generally, his mines consisted of an actuating device, either a manual or electric switch that would ignite a dozen boxes of buried dynamite. Some were rigged to go off if stepped on: a metallic rod extending an inch above ground would pierce a glass tube filled with high explosive that would in turn detonate a larger main charge. South African engineers disarmed or harmlessly detonated several hundred of these devices, and few actually did damage to the Union forces. Venuleth's efforts failed mostly because the locals compromised the mine locations to the Union forces as soon as the Germans departed the area, but many of the artisanal devices just failed to explode. Botha had a narrow escape himself when he and his staff rode over a mine that was detonated shortly afterwards by a lone horse. By the campaign's end, the South Africans would lose ten killed and twenty wounded to Venuleth's devices.[10]

During the night of 6 February, a South African patrol detonated one of his mines near Kilometer 4 of the *Otavibahn* rail line. The next morning, Captain Schultetus pushed two platoons forward to clarify the situation and was met by a major reconnaissance led personally by Colonel Skinner with the Imperial Light Horse. In the ensuing clash the Germans engaged a forward outpost and killed two Rhodesian troopers before retiring back up the Swakop. The Germans continued to harass the Allied forces from their camp at Felseneck further inland. The South Africans could observe the German patrols from atop the tower at the headquarters of the Woermann Line shipping company and tried to discourage them with the guns of the Royal Navy light cruiser HMS *Astraea* and a searchlight atop Swakopmund's lighthouse, but to no avail.

When the Germans abandoned Swakopmund they left it with a poisoned water supply. This angered General Botha enough on his arrival to write a formal protest letter to his adversary, Lieutenant Colonel Franke.[11] In a response that did not endear him to Botha, Franke stated that his troops had posted signs clearly warning of the danger and that it was not his fault if the enemy had overlooked them. Apparently, Franke did not understand the laws of land warfare or more likely, chose to interpret them rather loosely.

General Botha would use a cautious, measured approach to his campaign, although he had a personal tendency to expose himself to danger, much to the chagrin of Major Harry Trew, chief of his 100-man bodyguard unit. When chided by General Smuts that he should keep the general out of harm's way, Trew said he tried that often, but the general usually just told him to "go to hell."[12]

Knowing the campaign would be driven by the enormous logistical requirements to

9   Richard Hennig, *Deutsch-Südwest im Weltkrieg*, p.154; Victor Franke, *Tagesbuch: 1896-1920*, p.981; WS Rayner and WW O'Shaugnessy, *How Botha & Smuts Conquered German South West*, p.121.

10   Collyer, *The Campaign in German South West Africa*, p.141. Venuleth would help the South Africans locate and disarm the remaining mines following his surrender.

11   Botha took command on 11.2.1915; Franke was promoted on 20.1.1915.

12   W Whitthall, *With Botha and Smuts in Africa*, p.57.

UDF officers and men traveling on the newly built railway between
Walvis Bay and Swakopmund circa March 1915.(© Scientific Society
Swakopmund (Incorporated Association – not for Gain))

South African native laborers building the desert railway line
at Arandis. (© Namibian National Archives)

South African supply depot at KM 42 on Otavibahn east of
Swakopmund. (© Namibian National Archives)

feed the men and beasts of his army, a railway line had to be built to replace the dismantled
Otavibahn and the older, small-gauge *Staatsbahn* (state railway) that ran from Swakopmund
to Windhoek. First, a completely new line from Walvis Bay to Swakopmund was laid on
the shifting sands of the foreshore.[13] When that line was completed, the railway engineers
began to rebuild the *Otavibahn* that ran to Karibib and beyond. Botha expected this line
would serve to keep his forces supplied for the remainder of the campaign. As the work
crews inched eastward, a mixed brigade of light infantry and heavy artillery accompanied
them to provide security from expected German attacks. Several thousand black laborers
from South Africa toiled on the line, rebuilding it from the original German narrow gauge
(610mm / 2') to Cape Gauge (1,067mm / 3'6") under the supervision of white railway
engineers at a rate of about 1,000 meters per day.

The Northern Force was now in position to strike at the heart of German South West
Africa, but it was not until March 1915 that Botha assessed his troops to be prepared for
an advance.

Botha had several choices with the two best being either to push east from Swakopmund
along the *Otavibahn* or up the Swakop River Valley. The former offered a relatively easy
route, but one that left his mounted *Burghers* in open desert with little cover, water, or forage.
The Swakop River route would be a more difficult trek, but ideal maneuver terrain for his
cavalry. If he used the first route, Botha could count on the railway to supply his troops; on
the other he would require 400 wagons to support his advance along the river. His choice
was influenced by reports of ample rain in the central highlands; rain that would feed the

13   That rail line would later be rebuilt further inland, behind the dunes as the tides and wind quickly
undermined the sand bed under the track's sleepers.

ephemeral rivers and provide the South Africans with the water they needed to survive.

Additionally, the German's poor radio security gave the South Africans fairly precise intelligence that they faced enemy forces at Nonidas, Felseneck, and Goanikontes immediately to the east of Swakopmund.[14] In mid-February, Botha decided to eliminate these threats and consolidate his hold on the coast.

The Advance Begins

Lieutenant Colonel Franke visited the front on 17 February 1915 and finally decided it was time to take action. Four days later he ordered Major Wehle, who had taken over command from Weck in mid-January, to attack the "English."[15]

Wehle now had the 2nd Reserve Company, the 2nd Infantry Company, and the 3rd Reserve Battery at his disposal; a force that was not suitable for combined operations or attacking a superior force. With one mounted company, one dismounted, and an artillery battery equipped with outdated guns drawn by ponderously slow oxen, there was little Wehle could undertake against the enemy.

The matter was taken out of Wehle's hands when Botha's troops struck first on 23 February. With South African Colonel Brits in overall command, Colonel Skinner pushed forward with a mounted brigade through lightly defended Nonidas to attack Felseneck, while Colonel Alberts swung around Skinner's right flank to attack Goanikontes with a half brigade. The other half of the brigade under Colonel Commandant Collins went left to occupy the rail-line between Goanikontes and Rössing.

The Germans' first sign that something was amiss was the alarming vision of a large enemy cavalry force emerging from the early morning fog near their advance post at Nonidas. The *Kustenschutzabteilung* occupying Felseneck fell back precipitously and Schutetus, now outflanked on two sides, decided discretion was indeed the better part of valor. He directed his 200 troopers to fall back along the Swakop River by platoon. In leapfrog fashion, one platoon fell back as the next covered it from the high ground to the rear and only thus did the company withdraw and avoid being completely engulfed by *Burgher commandos*. Luckily for the Germans, one South African column got lost, having circled back on their start point, and never engaged in the fight. The Germans left behind 13 men, including one killed, and two severely wounded. Those who escaped regrouped the following day at Arandis near Kilometer 74 on the *Otavibahn*.

A surprise attack should have been anticipated. Schultetus believed an attack was imminent, but had one platoon positioned too far forward to be supported by the rest of his element. He himself was on patrol north of the Swakop River that morning with most of his men and narrowly escaped being overrun by three UDF mounted squadrons – an enemy force at least three times his strength.[16] Schultetus apparently did not anticipate the possibility of encirclement, despite knowing that the river valley could be accessed from its flanks as the South Africans ably demonstrated.

The South Africans now occupied Goanikontes, a small, comparatively lush oasis in the desert with a spring that provided good, if brackish water and surrounding fields with ample fodder for the animals and vegetables for the men. With this move, Botha had

---

14   Union Defense Force (UDF), *South Africa in the Great War 1914-1918: Official History*, pp.47-48.

15   For many Germans, the South Africans fighting against them were 'English.' Franke's operations order is quoted in Oelhafen, p.163.

16   KFH, 70.

occupied an important logistical point that would serve him for the advance through the Namib Desert. With two brigades ensconced at Nonidas and Goanikontes, the Union Army controlled the valley with mounted patrols as far as Heimgamchab and Rössing, 20 kilometers inland.

With his commitment to the Swakop, the wily Boer had revealed his intentions. Botha's presence alone was the strongest indicator that the northern approach would be the focus of the campaign. The South African move surprised and shook Franke enough that he finally abandoned his delusion that the northern approach was just a distraction. But even knowing the enemy's intentions, the German commander wavered. Franke's actions before the engagement at Felseneck and thereafter were indicative of the cautious and hesitant leadership he would display throughout the campaign to come.

The German defensive strategy had hinged on the expectation that the "English" would attack the protectorate directly across the southern border. General MacKenzie's landing at Lüderitzbucht had only reinforced that thinking. German troops manning border security posts in the southeast were also aware of South African preparations to cross the Kalahari from South Africa through Bechuanaland and into GSWA. Colonel Berrangé's pathfinders used pack animals and motor vehicles to place water and supplies in front of the advancing main body.[17] These supply dumps would enable the mounted troops of Eastern Force to survive the 400 kilometers crossing of the arid desert – a desolate expanse where the Germans had previously only employed camels and believed impassable with horses.[18]

MacKenzie had pushed forward from Lüderitzbucht to Tsaukaib where a large encampment and logistical base had been established. Meanwhile, Colonel van Deventer's Southern Force reoccupied Ramansdrift, which had been abandoned after Lukin's misadventure at Sandfontein the previous September. Absent the landings at Walvis Bay, the Germans would have been safe concentrating their forces in the South.

As the South African forces were gathering in the south, Austrian Lieutenant Paul Fiedler was flying overhead in his LFG Roland airplane. Fiedler was taking photographs and mapping the positions of the camps, while dropping the occasional bomb. His images are the only known aerial photographs in existence from the campaign.

With the capital of Windhoek and the north-south axis of the protectorate now threatened by Botha, Franke revised his strategy in an assessment written on 25 February. He now believed that the many avenues of advance open to a numerically superior enemy limited his options. He stated that, with the forces he had available at that moment, he would be forced to attack at any one of a number of chosen points to delay the South Africans, then withdraw and attack again at different point, which would quickly exhaust his troops and expose the most valuable region of the colony to the opponent.[19]

Far too late, he then decided to reinforce the "Right Wing" by ordering *Regiment Petter* forward to strengthen the line. That element had to travel by train from Kalkfontein-Süd. Its first elements arrived at Johann-Albrechtshöhe where it remained, 100 kilometers to the east and still too far to be of assistance to Major Wehle on the coast. Wehle also requested that *Regiment Naulila*, now under Captain Trainer, be deployed forward. Franke did not release that regiment immediately and they did not reach the front lines until 7 March when the 2nd and 6th Companies, the 1st Mountain-gun Artillery Battery, and *Halb*

---

17   Strachan, p.85.
18   Hennig, p.150.
19   KFH, 70; Oelhafen, p.165.

Batterie Weiherr arrived.

The Germans now faced the Union forces with four companies of infantry and two full and one half batteries of artillery, 12 guns in total. That included the 2nd Reserve Company, which remained at Arandis on the *Otavibahn* 40 kilometers away where it had withdrawn to after its escape from the valley several weeks before. It would not play a role in the upcoming fight.

Wehle decided to defend a line extending from Geiseb Mountains in the north across Pforte Mountain to the base of Langer Heinrich Mountain near a small farm and waterhole called Riet in the south. This would close the Swakop River Valley that ran from the coast up to the central highlands. He placed his command post to the rear at Jakalswater Station located eight kilometers east of Pforte and 14 kilometers north of Riet. Riet and Pforte could communicate with the commander by heliograph and telephones connected to the station along the old *Staatsbahn* railway lines. Signals from the two outstations were exchanged with a two-man heliograph detachment that was positioned on a promontory called the Walfischrucken or Whale Back about 800 meters south of Jakalswater station complex. A telephone was used to relay messages from that point to the commander. The only other form of communication was by mounted courier.

Wehle would place the 2nd Company and 2nd Infantry Company, along with the 3rd Reserve Battery at Riet. The 6th Company and *Halb Battery Weiherr* were placed forward at Pforte, while Wehle and his staff were at Jakalswater with the four guns of 1st Mountain-gun Artillery Battery (*Batterie Munstermann*) in reserve seven kilometers south at Modderfontein. All together Wehle's blocking force had about 670 men and 12 artillery pieces to cover a line approximately 25 kilometers wide. Franke visited Jakalswater on 16 March and approved Wehle's defensive plan with the exception of recommending to Weiherr that he pull the two-gun battery back to Jakalswater. Wehle did not agree, thinking the guns absolutely necessary to the defense of Pforte, and left them in position. Before he left, Franke cancelled his earlier order to attack Husab because he thought the *Schutztruppe's* horses needed to recuperate.[20] This would be one of the last opportunities to make an attack, as the odds against the Germans were about to change for the worse.

Meanwhile, Botha's primary concern was protecting the advanced supply depots along the Bay Road at Husab and the *Otavibahn* rail line. After the successful 23 February attack, he pushed his dismounted units including the Durban Light Infantry, Duke of Edinburgh's Own Rifles, 1st Transvaal Scottish, South African Irish, Rand Rifles, and the Witwaterrand Rifles, forward to Goanikontes, Heigamchab, and Husab as advance security. Along the railway, Skinner's dismounted infantry brigade, comprised of the 1st Rhodesian, 2nd Transvaal Scottish and 2nd Kimberley Regiments, was ordered to provide security for the rebuilding of that line as it inched along through the open desert about 40 kilometers north. Using some of the many motor trucks that had been shipped into Walvis Bay, tons of supplies were moving up the line to support the eventual advance. As the work moved along on the *Otavibahn* railway, a supply dump was placed behind the railhead to support the work in progress and moved forward as the construction proceeded.

Located 35 kilometers inland, at the foot of Husab Mountain south of Pforte Mountain, the Husab depot on the *Baaiweg* had an entirely different purpose.[21] It would support the

---

20   Oelhafen, p.172.
21   The Bay Road (*Baaiweg*) was the old wagon trail that linked the coast with the interior and ran more or less parallel to the south bank of the Swakop River.

7,500 South African troops as they moved up the river valley towards the German defenses. Doctor Henry Walker, a Royal Army Medical Corps officer assigned to the 3rd Mounted Brigade, related in his diary that some 1,625,000 pounds of supplies were being moved weekly to supply the forward forces. That included water and fodder for horses that could not be grazed on the parched desert, which Walker described as "a dreary plain, ... and not a blade of grass for [the animals] to eat."[22] The logistical requirements for both endeavors could not be sustained. Botha ordered railway construction, now at Kilometer 15 outside Swakopmund, to cease until the after the initial attack was made up the Swakop. And because transport was so scarce, the *commandos* were brought back to Swakopmund until early March to facilitate victualling the horses.[23]

As UDF Chief of Staff J.J. Collyer later wrote, Botha would capitalize on the *commandos'* mobility and try to repeat a victory similar to that of Scipio at Cannae, a double envelopment of the German positions at Pforte, Riet, and Jakalswater.

As the buildup began, the four-man German observation post high up on the peak of Langer Heinrich Mountain monitored the activity at the camp near Husab Mountain 30 kilometers to the west. Everything indicated Botha was making preparations for an advance. The South Africans were going all out to fill the depot with 5 and one half days of supplies for the push forward and the clouds of dust betrayed their movements. Still, the Germans did not investigate closely and did nothing to interdict or harass the enemy supply columns. In early March, the German estimate was that 800 Union troops were at Husab. [24]

On 19 March, the heliograph flashed its signal again – an even larger force had arrived at Husab.

Pforte, Riet, and Jakalswater

Botha's able Chief of Staff Colonel J.J. Collyer wrote the operations order for the successful advance on Heimgamchab and Goanikontes that took place on 22 February and placed the South African combat brigades in position for their subsequent moves.

Botha had a fairly clear picture of what he faced based on intelligence gleaned from poor German radio security coupled with the interrogation of prisoners. He believed the Germans had two 190-man mounted companies and a two-gun section of artillery at Pforte, along with four mounted companies and a battery of artillery at Riet. The reserve was thought to consist of two artillery batteries and four or five companies at Jakalswater and Modderfontein.[25] His estimates were generous, giving the Germans about 50 percent more strength than actually existed. Nevertheless, Botha was confident of success.

The German defense was actually three individual positions, each separated by a minimum of eight kilometers of difficult terrain. The most forward was at Pforte Mountain, a long, high ridge running generally north to south that was cut by three passes, called Eisenbahnpforte in the north, Weiße Pforte in the middle, and Husab Pforte in the south. The *Staatsbahn* rail line ran through the Eisenbahnpforte climbing the side of the mountain in a series of steep, tortuous switchbacks that required the train's passengers to

---

22   Henry F.B. Walker, *A Doctor's Diary in Damaraland*, IV.

23   Collyer, p.58. Sickness was also a serious problem among the animals as well as humans. Over 2,500 horses and mules suffering from glanders, a usually fatal bacterial disease, were destroyed by UDF veterinary personnel outside Swakopmund in late 1915.

24   Hennig, p.152.

25   UDF, p.48.

General Botha confers with his staff at Husab Camp before the battles of Pforte,
Riet, and Jakalswater on 18 March 1915. (© Namibian National Archives)

German troops moving by the *Staatsbahn* small gauge railway train (from
a pre-war postcard image). (© Namibian National Archives)

dismount and climb to the top of the pass on foot. That was before the war when the station on the west side of the pass sold beer and sausages.

There would eventually be two companies under the command of Captain Weiß. Initially, the 6th Company, *Kompanie Weiß*, with 190 rifles and two MG 08 machine-guns was in position at Weiße Pforte. On the north side of Eisenbahnpforte was the German connection to their headquarters at Jakalswater, *Lichtposten Pater*, equipped with a heliograph and a telegraph. On the southern side Sergeant Sanio and ten riflemen manned an observation post.

Wehle placed *Halb Batterie Weiherr* in the pass at Weiße Pforte, with the 6th Company providing close infantry support. Further to the south-west, near the end of the Pforte Mountain ridgeline, Lieutenant Bötticher and several troopers were posted to provide early warning of an enemy's approach.

The German position at Pforte was extremely vulnerable. Weiß was expected to hold a line 16 kilometers long with only 250 men and two cannon. Furthermore, his flanks to the south and north were unprotected and he had no safe line of withdrawal. If there was ever a position suited to ensure a soldier's last stand, this was it.

For his second major defensive position, Wehle chose a spot along the base of Langer Heinrich Mountain that lay astride the Bay Road. The road at this point passes along the north side of the mountain and continues towards the small farmstead and spring at Riet where it crosses the Swakop River. An excellent position, it was anchored on the southern side by the rocky 2,000 foot slope of the mountain and on the north by extremely difficult terrain of sharp, rocky kopjes and ridges along the banks of the Swakop River. Where the valley narrows to a point of best advantage to the defender – an open channel less than 1,500 meters wide – Wehle placed the 3rd Reserve Battery with its six FK 96 n/A artillery pieces and three venerable Maxim MG 08 machine-guns, along with two under-strength companies of infantrymen, the 2nd Infantry Company *Kompanie Ohlenschlager* and 2nd Company *Kompanie Watter* on a line perpendicular to the road. All together this force totaled only 200 rifles.

Major Wehle and his small staff was located to the rear at Jakalswater along with *Regiment Naulila* commander Captain Trainer and 25 armed men from the railway and post services. On top of the Walfischrucken two signalers manned the heliograph and field telephone connections to Riet and Pforte.

Wehle probably understood he was in an untenable position as Franke had failed to provide adequate reinforcements despite knowing that the Botha would advance up the Swakop River Valley. Wehle was attempting to defend without a reserve force and Franke's vague orders to "engage the enemy" left open how much resistance was to be offered. It would be up to Wehle to decide if he should simply delay the enemy or try to stop his advance completely.

A Second Wake-up Call

On 18 March 1915 at 0230 in the morning, Botha and his bodyguard of 100 South African Police moved forward and joined with the 5,000 troops of his two mounted brigades who camped at Nonidas and Goanikontes. As they arrived there late on the 18th, they "outspanned" and rested until 0630 the following morning when they rode forward and reached the Husab camp in the late morning. The Husab camp would be the last watering hole for 30 kilometers; the next was at Riet beyond the German defensive line.

At 1830 hours on the 19th, UDF troops saddled up once more to go into harm's way. The 2nd Mounted Brigade under Colonel Commandant J.J. Alberts headed north out of the camp along a track that would lead them to the Swakop River Valley. Beyond the dry riverbed, they would continue along the western base of the Husab Mountain heading for Pforte and the German positions 25 kilometers away. Colonel Coen Brits, the same man who wondered if he was to fight the English or the Germans, now led his 1st Mounted Brigade east along the Bay Road to meet his opponent. General Botha accompanied him with his 100 anxious bodyguards in tow.

On top of Langer Heinrich Mountain, Lieutenant Halsbrand signaled Jakalswater that enemy movement had been detected to the west. At Riet, 600 meters below the signal station and at Pforte, 20 kilometers to the northwest, the much smaller German force awaited the South Africans.

Stand to Arms.

Early on March 19th at Pforte, rifle fire was heard to the southwest. Shortly thereafter Lieutenant Bötticher and his element rode back into the lines. They had been chased off their forward OP by lead elements of Albert's brigade, the Ermelo and Standerton Commandos. Captain Weiß was now very aware the enemy was approaching and ordered his troops into battle positions.

Early in the morning of 20 March and at the very last moment, *Kompanie Steffen* arrived by train from Karibib.[26] After dropping a *Wachkommando* guard force of about 15 troopers at Jakalswater Station, Senior Lieutenant Steffen and 33 troops crossed the long open plain from Jakalswater by train to reinforce Captain Weiß. As soon as he arrived, Steffen was briefed on the situation and placed his men on the north side of Eisenbahnpforte. With Sanio and Pater's elements, Steffen commanded a total of 62 rifles. Steffen and his element were able to observe a large enemy contingent to the far west riding north towards Geiseb Mountain. This was Colonel Commandant Collins and 1,200 *Burghers* in five *commandos* and a scout unit heading for Jakalswater. Unable to engage, the Germans had to watch the massed cavalry pass and turn east in a cloud of dust that soon obscured them from view.

At Jakalswater, Major Wehle ordered Senior Lieutenant Neuhaus to check on the situation at Eisenbahnpforte and to return with the now empty train located there. He would end the day as a prisoner. Shortly before dawn, Wehle saw a large dust cloud in the still dark sky to the northwest of Jakalswater and thought Weiß had pulled his companies out of position precipitously. When the apparition was about 1,700 meters away, it was identified as a mass of enemy troops at least a thousand rifles strong. Against this onslaught, Captain Trainer ordered his 41 riflemen to covered positions on the eastern side of the raised railway bed and opened fire. Two UDF *commando* squadrons swung south behind the Walfischrucken hill and assaulted it. They first took the two signalers of the outpost atop the hill prisoner and then opened fire on the station below. By 0730, another 1,000 South Africans were in position around south, west, and north sides of the station at distances of 500 to 1,000 meters.

Strangely, the South Africans opened fire on the station from static positions in the desert surrounding the station, but did not wager an assault on the Germans. Instead

---

26   In February, the German staff assessed Steffen's 2nd Replacement Company to be suitable only for rear area defense and should not be employed on the front line except in an emergency; this was such a moment. KFH, p.74.

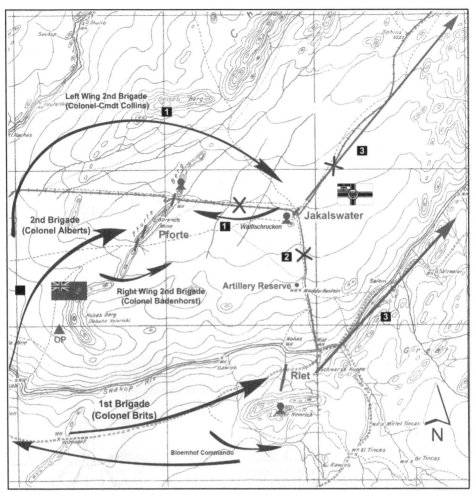

KEY

1. Collin's Advance & Retreat
2. Railway Demolition Points
3. German Lines of Withdrawal

/ German Defense & Movements
↗ Union Movements
♟ Signal Station

Overlay on Section of Union Defense Force General Staff Intelligence Special Map:
German S.W. Africa Swakop - Khan Rivers S.1
Topographic Section Ref. No. 107

General overview of Battles at Pforte, Riet, and Jakalswater,
19/20 March 1915. (© James Stejskal)

they poured rifle fire into the buildings, which was met with the *Schutztruppe's* carefully considered return fire. Collins' hesitance to attack was possibly influenced by the South African estimate that placed five companies and two artillery batteries at Jakalswater. The low level of return fire coming from the few Germans, however, would not have confirmed that belief.

At Pforte, Captain Steffen, now joined by Neuhaus, climbed through the pass to reconnoiter the plains that lay west of Pforte Mountain. In the dim early morning, they saw a second group of South Africans, from the Ermelo and Standerton Commandos, who arrived shortly after Collins' group passed. This group had taken artillery and machine-gun fire from Weiß' troops to the south and had swung further west to get out of range before swinging east to flank the north side of Eisenbahnpforte. Steffen alerted his small element and ordered them to fire as the *Burghers* came up the slopes on the north side of the pass. The *Burghers* were able to seize the pinnacle momentarily, but Steffen's deputy, Lieutenant Ewald, led a successful counterattack against the peak that regained the position, but he was killed in the assault. Steffen now realized there was a very large enemy force on the western slope. To the south at Weiße Pforte, the German artillery had just opened fire on the forces to their front. About 500 South Africans dismounted, leaving their horses on the plains below, and were climbing up the western slope between the two German companies.

Alberts' troops swarmed the German position like ants at a picnic. On the western slope, two *commandos* stormed the ridgeline and were threatening both Steffen's small company in the Eisenbahnpforte to the north and Weiß' company to the south. Further south, Swart's Scouts stormed through the southern-most pass at Husab Pforte. This was about the same time, 0630, as the Ermelo and Standerton Commandos were attacking Steffen's position. They were followed by Badenhorst and two *commandos*, which took control of the flat plains east of Pforte Mountain. What Steffen estimated to be 4-5,000 riders was in reality around 800 *Burghers*, at least until Collins' element joined the fray later in the morning after what would be an abortive raid on Jakalswater.

The four guns of the 4th Permanent Field Artillery also arrived west of Weiße Pforte and began a long-range duel with the two German guns. Captain Weiß saw his position threatened and pulled 6th company and Weiherr's guns out of the pass. Weiherr's battery could not keep pace with the company as they moved north on the east side of the mountain to the railway line. With the pass now clear, the South African artillery charged through and engaged the German guns from the rear. Weiherr had not made much progress because the mules pulling the guns were tired and the sand was deep. He met sustained rifle fire from Badenhorst's two commandos and was forced to deploy his guns in the open, firing to the east at Badenhorst's men. Weiß' 6th Company tried to provide covering fire from the ridgeline, but Weiherr was exposed and in serious trouble. Despite sustained rifle and artillery fire, he kept his gun crews firing. Emissaries were sent out on the orders of Colonel Alberts asking Weiherr to surrender. The lieutenant stubbornly refused, yelling back "As long as I have ammunition and cannoniers, it's out of the question!"[27] At one point during the battle, Commandant Piet Botha wandered off the hill mistakenly believing the guns were South African and into the position. Realizing his mistake, Botha tried to bluff his way out by demanding the crews give up. In the confusion of dust and gunfire, Botha made his escape before the Germans could capture him.[28] Finally, nearly out of ammunition,

---

27 Oelhafen, p.177.
28 UDF, p.42; L'Ange, p.186.

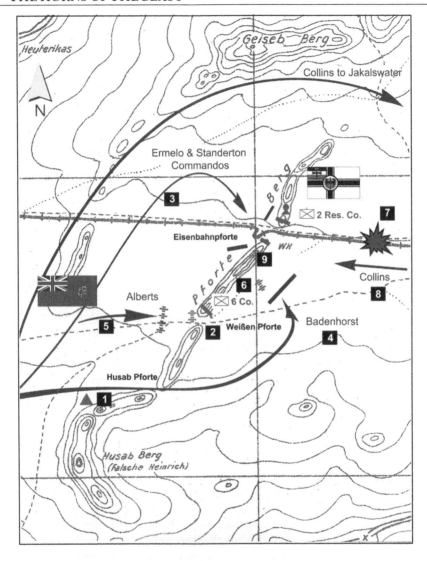

1. OP (LT v. Bötticher) southwest of Husab Pforte driven back by UDF on 19 March

2. 0600 - Initial position of Half Battery Weiherr at Weißen Pforte (2 x FK 96 n/A)

3. 0600 - Ermelo & Standerton Commandos (Alberts) begin assault

4. Colonel Badenhorst penetrates Husab Pforte to encircle and prevent German retreat

5. Main Body follows up with Permanent Field Artillery (4 x QF 13pdrs) through Weiße Pforte

6. 0800 - Weiherr's Battery out of action. Weiherr KIA, crews wounded or dead, Guns captured.

7. German troop train put out of action, engine burned.

8. Colonel Commandant Collins joins battle after being forced off Jakalswater

9. 1200 - 6.Company (Weiß) surrenders, 1400 - 2 Replacement Company (Steffen) surrenders

Overlay on Section of Union Defense Force General Staff Intelligence Map:
Sheet 1. German S.W. Africa Swakop - Khan Rivers
Topographic Section Ref. No. 107

Detailed view of movements and action at Battle of Pforte. (© James Stejskal)

Weiherr was hit by rifle fire and went down, dead. By that time, the battery's gun-crews were all wounded or dead and the South Africans were able to capture the two guns intact.

While the Germans were fighting for their lives, the train that had brought Steffen to Pforte tried to return to Jakalswater but found that Swart's Scouts cut the rail line. The train was quickly surrounded. After the crew was removed, the train was burned and Pforte was cut off completely.

At Riet, the patrols sent forward towards Husab on the 19th were forced to fall back on the main defensive line by Brits' advance. At 0430, Krüger ordered everyone into battle positions. A battery of six guns, behind 200 riflemen and three Maxims all in prepared firing positions, awaited the order to fire. The right flank of the line was grounded at the Swakop River where another platoon of infantry under Lieutenant Tesch sat behind wire obstacles and mines placed in the riverbed.

Colonel Brits sent several Scout units forward on a reconnaissance straight up the Bay Road and tasked Commandant Bezuidenhout's Bloemhof Commando, a squadron of 300 troops, to flank south of Langer Heinrich in hope of finding the Tincas River Pass that would bring them around behind the Germans. Although the sought-after pass was depicted on his map, Bezuidenhout could not find it and gave up, returning all the way to Husab Camp without bothering to inform his commander. Had he found it, the *commando* would have emerged about three kilometers behind the Germans and been in position to attack from the rear or cut off any withdrawal. Now, Brits was left to wonder what had become of Bezuidenhout.[29]

At 0600, Krüger was with the guns and observed the first enemy patrol to his right front. Fifteen minutes later, he ordered the six 7.7cm guns of the 3rd Reserve Battery to open fire, which pinned the *Burgher* scouts down in a ravine 1,000 meters to the German front. They would remain there for most of the day. About the same time, the 2nd Company opened fire on dismounted troops that appeared to their front. The main body of seven *commandos* – about 2,100 troopers – appeared under a dust cloud 4,000 meters away at 0700. Kruger gave the general order to open fire and the South Africans immediately replied with the four QF 13-pounders of the Transvaal Horse Artillery and machine-guns. For the next two and a half hours, a gun duel took place, but the Germans took the brunt of the fire. The German observation post on Langer Heinrich had been seen by the South Africans and took direct fire, forcing them to find cover. Captain Haußding, a reservist with only minimal experience, was now without a forward observer to direct his guns' fire. Although he believed he was on the mark, his battery was overshooting the Union positions and causing little damage. The Union artillery was firing from just behind the ridgeline and their resulting plunging fire was more effective. Nevertheless, the Germans continued to return fire. Krüger called Major Wehle to request the support of the 1st Mountain-gun Artillery Battery, but it had already begun to move north to Jakalswater where the need was more pressing.

Brits's frontal assault stalled about 2,700 meters before the German lines. The *Burghers* dismounted in front of the artillery and were exchanging rifle fire with the *Reiter* who were well protected in their *Schützengraben* (firing positions) scraped out of the desert sand and fronted with granite boulders. It was the German artillery that suffered the most. A direct hit on a limber tore it to shreds and killed its oxen. In all, three wagons and two limbers

---

29   J.J. Collyer claimed that the pass was possibly a figment of the cartographer's imagination, however, its
      position is very accurately depicted on the UDF's S.1 intelligence map. Collyer, p.69.

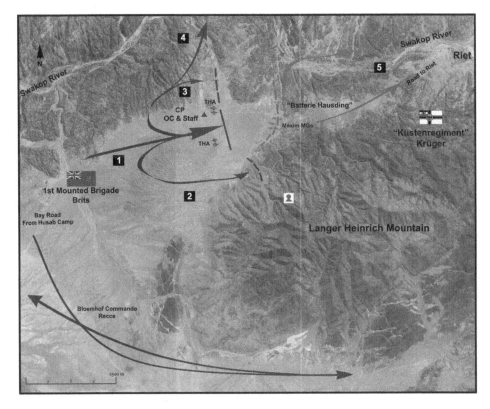

BRITS' ASSAULT AT RIET
20 March 1915

1. Brits' Line of March
2. Right Wing First Attempt to Flank
3. Left Wing Attempt to Flank - Final Assault 1330
4. Brinks Attempt to Flank
5. German Withdrawal
⚓ Mines
👤 German Signal Troop

Map and Data by J.Stejskal & J.Kinahan

Detailed view of movements and action at Battle of Riet. (© James Stejskal)

would be destroyed by Union artillery fire, but none of the guns were put out of action.

Brits decided to flank the German position and sent a *commando* against the German left, up the slopes of Langer Heinrich. An additional squadron followed and initially made some progress, but soon stalled in the difficult terrain. Major Brink, Brits' Brigade Major was sent to reconnoiter in the opposite direction; his mission was to find a flanking route on the north side of the river. Brink and his forces entered the dry Swakop riverbed, but sheer rock walls on the far side stymied them and their assault could make no headway. Brits' attack languished and by late afternoon the Union forces stopped their advance approximately 1,000 meters to the west of the German lines. In his description of the battle, Collyer asserts that Brits wasted time by waiting for the Bloemhof Commando to appear behind the Germans and should have attacked the German flank closest to the mountain to dislodge them and trap the artillery against the foothills.[30] That General Botha did not over-ride his subordinate and order such a move is probably testament to Colonel Brit's good judgment. At the point of the German defense line, the valley was extremely narrow and a frontal assault would have left Brits' men exposed to close range, enfilade artillery and machine-gun fire that probably would have blunted any attack and cost the South Africans many lives.

At Jakalswater, Colonel Commandant WR Collins' troops cut the railway lines just west and north of Jakalswater and then settled into positions covering the station on three sides. With the South Africans pouring down fire on them, the Germans were pinned down and in a precarious position. Fortuitously for the Germans, at the outset of the battle, Wehle telephoned Major Munstermann, commander of the reserve artillery at Modderfontein, to request his support. Gregor Proppe, the battery veterinarian, later related that the battery's troops had already heard the gunfire and were preparing to move. The 120-man mountain-gun battery, augmented by a 50-man infantry platoon, received its "alert" at 0600 and was rolling north minutes later. Leaving behind their baggage wagons, the unit covered six kilometers before taking rifle fire from South Africans on top of the Walfischrucken about 1,500 meters to their front.

Around 0630, the four-gun battery unlimbered and began to fire on the promontory, but Munstermann decided the chance of overshooting the hill and hitting the station was too great, so he displaced to the east and began to shell the position again from a distance of 500 meters.[31]

The 200 *Burghers* on the hill were now taking heavy enfilade fire from the guns and riflemen. The red-hot shrapnel singing past their ears was one danger for the *Burghers*, the rifle bullet ricochets and splintering granite were quite another. The hill turned into a hot spot and during a lull in the fire, German Captain Vorberg led an infantry assault on the backside of hill. His element completely surprised the South Africans. During the raid, the Germans captured 28 *Burghers* with 40 horses and freed their comrades. At that moment, a mass of riders tore off to the west on their horses from behind the hill; it was the first sign of the *Burghers'* weakening resolve. Once more, Munstermann relocated his battery, this time to the north side of the station where he could direct fire against the South Africans who were lying in the open. Around 1000 hours, Collins decided Jakalswater was too hot for his liking and withdrew all his troops to the west. He gave up too soon as the defenders' ammunition was nearly exhausted. After the withdrawal Collins' troops augmented those

30 Collyer, p.68.
31 Dr Gregor Proppe, *Erinnerungen eines sehr alten Tierarztes*, pp.49-52.

Collins' Attack on Jakalwater
20 March 1915

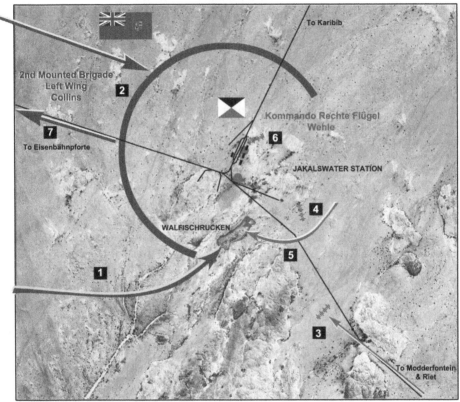

1. Initial advance of Collins Commandos, Walfishrucken occupied circa 0600.
2. Collins Main Force arrives, establishes perimeter, Station under attack.
3. German 1st Mountain Battery arrives 0630, initial firing position at 1,200 meters.
4. Second firing position at range of 500 meters.
5. German infantry counterattacks, re-occupies Walfishrucken.
6. Final position of 1st Mountain Battery.
7. Withdrawal of Collins towards Pforte.

● German Defenses

⚇ Signal Station

Detailed view of movements and action at Battle of Jakalswater. (© James Stejskal)

Jakalswater Station as it appeared circa 1905. (Original
photographer unknown) (© James Stejskal)

of Badenhorst in their assault against Captain Weiß' 6th Company and Lieutenant Steffens'
2nd Company at Pforte. But they nearly met with grief as they rode onto the plains near
Pforte. Collins failed to warn Badenhorst of his approach and his squadrons almost came
under "friendly" fire.[32] It was another instance of poor communications between UDF
elements, an aspect that would need improvement as the force matured.

Collins later claimed he had briefly taken the station and a train full of reinforcements,
but abandoned both when the artillery fire became too intense.[33]

The Germans' small victory at Jakalswater could only be celebrated for a short moment.

After Weiherr's battery was put out of action, the South Africans redirected their
artillery fire against the 6th Company. Weiß decided his position was untenable and
ordered his troops to destroy the two machine-guns and their rifles, which were thrown
onto the rocks below. Around midday, he surrendered his veteran company that fought
successfully at Sandfontein and Naulila.

Several kilometers to the north, Steffen's small detachment fought on for another two
hours before the sustained rifle and artillery fire brought him to the same conclusion. Before
then, the signal detachment on the north side of Eisenbahnpforte made heliograph contact
with the re-established post on the Walfischrucken at Jakalswater. At 1115 the message
came: "We are fully surrounded", ten minutes later: "Company and battery captured" –
meaning the 6th Company.[34] At 1400, Steffen surrendered his small detachment, the last
of the Pforte defenders.

---

32   Collyer, p.73.
33   L'Ange, p.187. Interestingly, German accounts do not mention that Collins' incursion came close to the
     station and, while archaeological surveys have established the UDF position on the Walfischrucken, there
     is no comparable evidence the South Africans pressed their attack forward into the station at any location.
34   Oelhafen, p.163.

Although the signal post on the Walfischrucken continued to attempt contact, Wehle soon had no doubt that the entire Pforte Mountain line had been captured, putting both Jakalswater and Riet in danger of envelopment. Wehle had telegraphed Franke in Windhoek to alert him of Botha's attack that morning. Franke responded by sending *Regiment Petter* forward to reinforce Wehle from its laager at Johann Albrechts-Höhe 100 kilometers to the rear. Petter's regiment was, however, too far away and too late to be of any assistance. The lack of a reserve at Jakalswater and thin line of defenders at Pforte doomed the German position there from the outset. It is probable that Franke assumed Botha's assault would not be in force – he was wrong.[35]

At 1230, Wehle sent Krüger the news that Pforte had fallen and his element at Jakalswater would withdraw. He ordered Krüger to conduct a fighting retreat eastwards up the Swakop River to the waterhole at Salem and then to continue on to Kubas. At 1330, Krüger's right wing, including Lieutenant Tesch's blocking platoon on the Swakop, turned back one last Union assault, after which the South Africans pulled back to rest. Earlier that day, the signal station on Langer Heinrich advised Krüger that the Bloemfeld Commando was flanking south of Langer Heinrich. In response he had taken two platoons from the 2nd Infantry Company and placed them to his rear covering the Bay Road. These would now cover his withdrawal, which began after the artillery exchanges died down around 1600. Krüger was able to quietly and carefully withdraw his troops from their positions even while still under artillery fire. They moved back to their supply depot at Riet to regroup and moved on in the early evening, leaving behind a small detail to blow up the supplies. The Union Forces did not follow, having failed to notice that the Germans had withdrawn. The next morning, Brits renewed his attack only to find the defenders had disappeared.

Wehle sent out reconnaissance patrols after Collins' force had retired from Jakalswater. They returned to report that very heavy enemy forces were present around Pforte and a strong patrol was observed to the south riding towards Modderfontein. This element was also noted by Krüger's forces at Riet and caused some concern during the withdrawal.

Wehle had felt it pointless to risk sending the 1st Mountain-gun Artillery Battery forward to assist with the defense of Pforte. After repairing the rail line, a train was dispatched to Karibib with the wounded and those without mounts. While Krüger was beginning his move to the rear, Wehle pulled the force off Jakalswater towards Karibib and then to Kubas.

The Germans made another serious error when Major Munstermann chose to abandon the wagons his battery had left behind at Modderfontein. When the South Africans later searched the site, they found a trove of documents that showed the main body of the *Schutztruppe* to be in the north, as well as a map showing locations of Venuleth's mines in the river valley. This windfall provided Botha the intelligence he needed to order MacKenzie to immediately advance from Tschaukaib in the south.[36]

The next day, Wehle sent a reconnaissance patrol from Karibib by train as far as Jakalswater to look for stragglers and wounded. Other mounted patrols from Captain Schultetus' company at Arandis went as far as Pforte and Riet to find the Union forces absent from the battlefield. A number of stragglers without mounts who had evaded the South African patrols were also picked up. A hospital train was intercepted by a troop of South Africans, but allowed to pass when its purpose was determined to be humanitarian.

---

35   KFH, p.77.
36   Collyer, p.77.

South African *commandos* surround the wreckage of *Schutztruppe* Lieutenant Weiherr's Half Battery after the battle at Pforte on March 20, 1915. The Weiße Pforte is at center rear. (© Scientific Society Swakopmund (Incorporated Association – not for Gain))

UDF officers confer over German Model 96 n/A guns captured at Pforte from Weiherr's half battery. (© Namibian National Archives)

After the battles, *Regiment Naulila* was dissolved. The Germans now had two companies of 400 rifles total and two artillery batteries to oppose the 7,500 South African troops in front of them. *Regiment Petter* arrived near Karibib on 22 March and brought the *Schutztruppe* force up to five companies and three artillery batteries, but they were still hopelessly outnumbered. Franke feared that a drive by Botha would soon cut the north-south railway and threaten Windhoek in the center of the country. That would drive a wedge between the German forces in the north and those remaining in the south and prompted Franke to plan for their unification. Franke was again responding to enemy actions rather than anticipating them.

On 20 March, the South Africans won the day. Their losses were 13 killed and 41 wounded against the Germans 20 dead and 19 wounded. But the Germans lost 277 prisoners compared to 28 Union troops captured. Those losses, along with the two guns captured, were irreplaceable for the *Schutztruppe*. The Union forces had demonstrated their abilities to overcome difficult terrain and endure hardship. Botha's decision not to tie his advance to the *Otavibahn* rail line permitted his *commandos* to exploit their maneuverability in classic form, much to the detriment of the Germans who were hobbled in their ability to respond by a hesitant commander. Had the Germans held out for a full day the South Africans might have been forced to break off their attack, so much hinged on the capture of the wells and the water necessary to sustain Botha's forces.

As it was, the long, hard ride before the battle, along with the heat and little available water, meant both men and horse were spent. The predicted grass did not appear at Riet and the water in the local springs was not enough to sustain a force of 7,500 troops. Botha was forced to withdraw his cavalry to Swakopmund where they could be supplied from ships. The Durban Light Infantry was moved up to garrison Riet and Jakalswater along with one *commando* squadron to conduct security patrols in the area. Meanwhile, the logistics build up for the next push forward began anew.

In the South

Botha's occupation of the Riet – Jakalswater line precipitated the complete German withdrawal from the extreme south. This took place in two phases. First, Franke ordered units of the southern border to proceed to the southern edge of the Karrasberg Mountains. The Germans pulled back from a wide arc that covered the central south to establish a defense line to slow the South African advance.

Opposing the approximately 800 *Schutztruppe* in the south was the Central Force of General MacKenzie with three mounted brigades and two six-gun artillery batteries (1,800 rifles) approaching Aus, Colonel van Deventer's Southern Force with 29 *commandos* and one artillery battery (5,000 rifles), and Colonel Berrangé's Eastern Force with four mounted regiments and one heavy artillery battery (1,200 rifles). Another seven infantry regiments (5,000 rifles) were deployed behind MacKenzie along the Lüderitzbucht railway as rear area security troops. After his victory at Pforte and Riet, Botha traveled south to Lüderitzbucht to meet with MacKenzie on 29 March. According to Gerald L'Ange, Botha was frustrated with MacKenzie's lack of progress on Aus and ordered him to advance.[37] Shortly thereafter, General Smuts was given command of the Southern Force, which now consisted of MacKenzie's 1st Division and van Deventer and Berrangé's combined forces in

---

37   L'Ange, p.207.

the 2nd Division after they united at Kabus on 20 April.

On 22 March, Franke ordered the evacuation of Aus and the heavily fortified town was abandoned. An assault on Aus would have been a difficult nut for the South Africans to crack, but the defenders feared being cut-off from their withdrawal route north with van Deventer and Berrangé's forces converging to their rear. The German forces would regroup at Keetmanshoop and continue north to meet up with the bulk of the *Schutztruppe*. The pull back was not without incident; a number of skirmishes took place. The Germans often stayed in close contact with the Union forces to monitor their advance. More than once small German patrols were overwhelmed by larger Union forces and put out of action. The actions were not one sided and Union forces suffered losses as well, as they met with tenacious resistance until contact was broken or the situation became hopeless and the Germans surrendered.

MacKenzie was now moving north-east towards Bethanie and Berseba following the Germans. By mid-April, the Germans converged on Keetmanshoop and then moved towards Gibeon with the last train leaving on 19 April.

Captain von Kleist commanded the rear guard as the Germans pulled back. He was not an experienced tactician and his poor judgment would lead to several unnecessary and bloody encounters. His subordinate officers regarded him as authoritarian and unwilling to consider the opinions of other officers.[38] There were a number of small skirmishes as von Kleist directly engaged the Union advance forces rather than withdraw his greatly outnumbered forces unmolested. These engagements were unnecessary as the South Africans were not yet able to threaten his force. Further, the land over which the Germans were moving was not suitable for defense; open and with little vegetation it was ideal for fast moving mounted units once the opponents were in contact. Two skirmishes at Kabus and Berseba on 23 April cost both time and manpower. While the Union forces lost a few men killed and taken prisoner in the two battles, the Germans lost three killed, a number of wounded, and 11 prisoners.[39] MacKenzie kept moving north while von Kleist lost more irreplaceable resources.

Von Kleist's main force, some 800 rifles, managed to break free and arrived in Gibeon on 25 April. The commander was convinced the enemy was not within striking distance and set up camp eight kilometers east of the town near the rail station, thinking his troops could get a day's rest before continuing. Once again, poor communication security coupled with a commander's decisions would lead to disaster.

In the night of 26 April, MacKenzie pushed forward, encouraged by intelligence intercepts of the German railway telegraph that had not been cut in the south. He now knew a German force along with a train full of supplies was located at Gibeon and did not anticipate his presence – he was much closer than von Kleist could imagine.

MacKenzie sent a team of scouts and engineers to sabotage the rail two miles north of Gibeon to prevent the train's departure. Behind them followed Lieutenant Colonel J.R. Royston and the 9th Mounted Brigade and an element of the 8th. Royce was to be positioned along the rail-line to block a German withdrawal when the main force attack came the next morning, but he chose a site too close to the Germans that had no cover. The Germans were alerted to the presence of the enemy by machine-gun fire and detonations

---

38   Hennig, p.176.
39   The Germans tended to leave their wounded behind on the battlefield as they could not provide adequate care during the withdrawal.

north of the station and, when a patrol discovered Royston's force, they reacted swiftly to contain the intruders. Several hours of combat ensued and in the early morning, Royston's troops found themselves outgunned and in a precarious position. Royston withdrew east under pressure but left one squadron of the Natal Light Horse surrounded. The South Africans had thus far lost 24 killed, 50 wounded, and 130 captured.

Von Kleist had by this time arrived on a scene of celebration as the Germans happily congratulated themselves and were in the process of breaking up their opponents' captured weapons. The celebration was premature, however. MacKenzie was about to break up the party with his main force that had gone unnoticed by the Germans. Among other failures, von Kleist had failed to set advance pickets to warn of an enemy approach. Now, without these, the German position was about to be attacked from the south by a far superior force. MacKenzie threw a squadron straight at the station while other squadrons rode right and left of the objective. With superiority in men and artillery (six guns to two) the South Africans forced von Kleist into a fighting retreat. The German train was sitting at the station under full steam but surrendered as soon as the Union artillery fired on it – several tons of explosives on board apparently made the train crew nervous. The prisoners were soon abandoned, their guards unable to herd the men and return fire at the same time. Royston was able to salvage some of his dignity as he rode back into battle from the north-east to help with the rout. The pursuit continued for twenty miles, the Germans kept good order while Union cavalry tried unsuccessfully to outflank them over the rough, rock-strewn terrain. By nightfall, MacKenzie called it off as his men and horses were exhausted after 16 days of movement from Aus. Von Kleist kept two-thirds of his troops but lost a valuable train with its crew and many supplies, two cannon, 11 dead, and about 190 captured. Their salvation was Royston's failure to properly set his blocking force in position.

While the escaping Germans continued their trek north to join their comrades, the UDF's Southern Army was disbanded on 5 May 1915. Four regiments of Union dismounted infantry went north to augment Botha along with Colonel van Deventer. The war in the south was over.

The Glorious Basters

Unlike other German colonies, the *Schutztruppe* in South West Africa did not make heavy use of native troops other than in support roles such as drovers, general laborers, and personal servants called *Bambusen*. There were a few exceptions, including the Rehoboth Baster, a people of mixed heritage, the result of unions between Cape Colony Dutch or "Boer" and the indigenous Namaqua peoples who first emerged in northern Cape Colony in the 18th Century. Called *Mischlinge* by the Germans, the Basters crossed the Orange River into SWA around 1868 to establish themselves as an independent society at Rehoboth, which today lies 90 kilometers south of the capital of Windhoek.

The Basters had concluded a protection treaty with the colonial authority in 1885 that left them in autonomous control of their territory, an area of just over 14,000 square kilometers south of Windhoek; a special status achieved by no other indigenous tribe or ethnic group in the colony. As part of their treaty, the Basters provided troops to serve alongside the *Schutztruppe* as needed. They filled this requirement well, with an approximately 150-man Baster Company fighting on the side of the Germans against the Herero in 1896 and against the Bondelswarts, on the border with the Cape Colony, in 1903. They were employed against Herero in the front lines at the Battle of Waterberg in

1904, which marked the end of the Herero uprising. It was a sign of the supreme trust the Germans placed in the Basters, as all other indigenous peoples with the force were relegated to unarmed, second echelon support roles.

Nevertheless, the "good" relations the Basters had with the German community began to unravel as more colonists arrived in the territory. The colonial administration was exhorted by the settlers to end the special status the Basters held in the hopes of acquiring their valuable land. The measures taken against the Basters were meant to enforce the "rule of difference" that kept the indigenous peoples on a lower level than the white settlers and were even more stringently enforced following the Herero and Namaqua uprisings.[40]

In early August 1914, Heydebreck gave the order to reconstitute the Baster Company, which had been dormant since the end of the 1908 Namaqua uprising. At the same time, the other indigenous groups were isolated and put under watch to ensure they remained quiet during the anticipated conflict.

The Basters were at first reluctant to be called up citing their lack of readiness along with their unwillingness to be caught up in a "European War" between whites. They were also reluctant to fight against the Afrikaner with whom they had a common language and heritage. The local German commander in Rehoboth, the Baster capital, was able to convince the Basters that their duties would not place them in combat against whites and after several weeks of refresher training the company was operational.

The Baster Company was deployed under German officers to conduct reconnaissance in the Namib Desert around the British enclave of Walvis Bay and to curb the activities of criminal bands that were ranging out of the enclave towards the German port town of Swakopmund.

When Union commander General Botha occupied the central coast, *Schutztruppe* commander Franke made a fateful decision to pull the Basters back and to utilize them to guard the Union Prisoners of War (POW) at a camp near Uitdrai. The Basters were upset with this arrangement as it took them out of their territory and placed them in direct contact with the South Africans with whom they were allied by language and blood. The Basters were also intimidated by the prisoners' threats of retribution against them once the war was over. As the relationship between guards and prisoners became closer, the Basters began to assist some of the South Africans to escape. Other Basters simply deserted. When the POW camp at Uitdrai was moved further north to Otjiwarango, the Baster council decided to refuse to guard the camp. To do so, they feared, would demonstrate they were not neutral in the conflict.

As it became clear to the Basters that the Germans were losing, many of the younger members of the tribe saw an opportunity to seek an alliance with the South Africans. A Baster leader, Nels van Wyk (also known as Cornelius), made his way secretly through the Namib Desert from Rehoboth to Swakopmund to meet with General Botha on 1 April 1915. In the first meeting, van Wyk informed Botha that the Basters did not stand with the Germans and intended to rise up against them. According to South African records, Botha allegedly counseled van Wyk not to rise up but to await the Union forces that were

---

40   The rule of difference exists in a divide between groups, in this case settlers and indigenous peoples who live in the same geographical area. When the superior group refuses to permit the lesser group's assimilation, the governing principle is known as the rule of difference. See George Steinmetz, *The Devil's Handwriting: Precoloniality and the German Colonial State in Qingdao, Samoa, and Southwest Africa*, p.36.

now making their way up from the south towards Rehoboth. The only surviving first-hand record is a cable Botha sent General J.C. Smuts that stated van Wyk and the Basters were "well disposed" towards the South African government.[41] Baster traditional accounts, however, state that Botha supported an uprising.[42] The South African account contrasts with that of the official German after-action report, which recounts that van Wyk met with Botha on 1 April and left Swakopmund on 14 April with two ox wagons, probably loaded with arms and ammunition.[43]

As the German situation deteriorated and Baster desertions increased, Governor von Seitz asked the Basters to surrender their weapons with the promise they would be left alone. The disgruntled Basters had made their decision, however, and the die was cast. Following the return of van Wyk, the situation in Rehoboth rapidly spiraled out of control. The Baster council had lost its influence and was unable to convince the younger Basters to give up their weapons. Van Wyk called for revolt. It began during the night of 17/18 April with the desertion of all the Basters from the POW camp at Uitdrai and the flight of two Baster guards from a *Schutztruppe* horse kraal with their weapons. News that a German soldier had shot the two deserters spread through the community and the uprising gained momentum. Van Wyk ordered the murder of several local German police officers and farmers who had their property within Basterland; the German High Command responded with a declaration of war against the Basters on 22 April. After the last attempt at negotiations was made, it was clear that the Baster council was powerless to control the uprising. A company of *Schutztruppe* mounted infantry with attached machine-gun platoons and artillery were sent to Rehoboth primarily to safeguard the German residents and the Police detachments. Simultaneously, troops retiring from Keetmanshoop in the south came streaming into Rehoboth. The mission rapidly changed as the German operational commander, Captain Graf von Saurma-Jeltsch, expecting to meet a massed enemy, instead met dispersed guerrilla bands. The Basters had proven themselves fighting the Herero and Nama guerrillas and now had employed the same tactics against a superior military force.

When the Germans sent out troops to disarm the Basters, the situation was further enflamed and shots exchanged. Most of the Baster population then deserted their homes and headed for a village called Sam Kubis in the mountains about 50 kilometers to the south-west of Rehoboth.

By sending out reconnaissance troops, von Saurma was able to detect some lucrative targets and moved to eliminate them. The Basters' weakness was an attachment to their cattle herds as the accompanying dust clouds gave away their movements. Nevertheless, while the Germans were able to engage several small Baster elements, the majority – some 700-800 people – managed to reach the sanctuary of the mountainous heights at Sam Kubis, a rugged area that provided cover and was difficult to access from the canyons below. On 8 May, German troops closed in on Sam Kubis and engaged the Baster with two companies, a platoon with three Maxim machine-guns, and a half-battery with two cannon. Throughout the day, the Germans battered the position from an adjacent hilltop

---

41   G.J.J. Oosthuzen, "The Military Role of the Rehoboth Basters during the South African Invasion of German South West Africa, 1914-1915," *Scientia Militaria*, 96.

42   There is no evidence to suggest Botha did support the uprising, which would have been in opposition to standing South African Government policies toward coloured peoples.

43   Oelhafen, p.147.

with the battle ceasing only at nightfall. The Baster had suffered greatly losing 17 men in one fighting position alone, but the situation changed dramatically the next morning.

On 9 May, a German patrol delivered the news to Graf von Saurma that the Union forces under General MacKenzie were approaching Rehoboth and he made the decision to terminate the attack. Pulling back, von Saurma was forced to go cross-country to avoid not only MacKenzie's forces, but those of General Botha who had closed in on Windhoek, in order to join up with the German main force in the north.

The Basters began to return to their homes, but took revenge on any of the remaining German farmers by killing those they found and looting the homesteads of those absent. For the Basters, the break-off of the attack was seen as the intervention of God. For the Germans, it was a mission unfinished.

Trekkopje

In late April 1915, the UDF railhead was at Kilometer 81 on the *Otavibahn*, between the two whistle stops of Arandis and Ebony, heading towards Karibib. General Botha was continuing his buildup of supplies at Riet for the push to Windhoek, while laborers were toiling on the rail-line. One kilometer behind the railhead, the UDF's 3rd Infantry Brigade was providing security. It was encamped at a god-forsaken station in the desert called Trekkopje. The 3rd was commanded by newly promoted General P.C.B. Skinner and consisted of the ILH, the 2nd Kimberley, and 2nd Transvaal Scottish Regiments. Sitting 15 kilometers to the rear at Arandis was the 1st Rhodesian Regiment along with one Armstrong BLC 15-pdr anti-aircraft gun called "Skinny Liz."

As the rail line inched forward from Swakopmund, blockhouses, each manned by an officer or senior sergeant and six men, were built alongside to provide security. It was an effective deterrent well learned from the British during the second Boer War. The troopers

Schutztruppe formation at Karibib. (© Namibian National Archives)

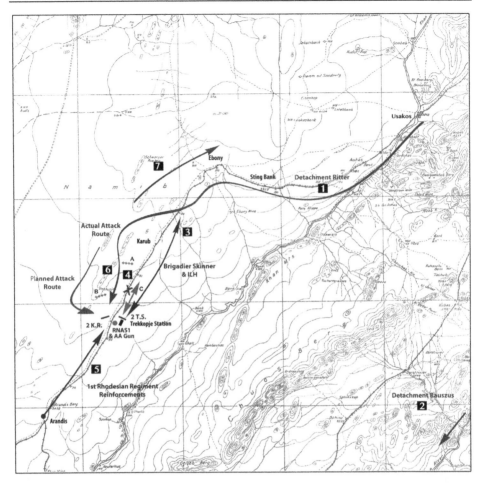

Battle of Trekkopje Overview
26 April 1915

1. Ritter's Schutztruppe force move during night of 25 /26 April to attack Trekkopje.
2. Major Bauszus marches towards Salem & Riet as diversion.
3. Skinner's Scouts spot Schutztruppe columns at 0100, return to base.
4. Schutztruppe enginners detonate railway charges at 0500.
5. 1st Rhodesian Rifles move to reinforce Trekkopje, arrive 0710.
6. Ritter's artillery opens fire at 0700, attack begins, last company committed 0800.
7. Attack falters, Ritter orders withdrawal at 0900.

A. First firing position of 1st & 2nd Mountain-gun Batteries, Range 4,300 meters.
B. Second firing position, Range 1,500 meters.
C. RNAS No 1 armoured cars provide machine-gun support to defenders.

Overlay on Section of Union Defense Force General Staff Intelligence Map:
Sheet 1. German S.W. Africa Swakop - Khan Rivers
Topographic Section Ref. No. 107

Detailed view of movements and action at Battle of
Trekkopje, 26 April 1915. (© James Stejskal)

of the brigade were also relegated to outpost duty far to the front of the railhead as early warning posts.

All the Union supplies came forward by train from Swakopmund, an irregular service guided more by breakdowns than schedules. The terrain around Trekkopje was open ground punctuated by scrub, rock outcroppings and kilometers of nothingness. It was an ideal location for an attacker; less so for anyone to defend, let alone be posted at. Skinner had just lost his heavy artillery, two QF 12-pdr 18 cwt naval guns modified for land use that were pulled back to the coast.

After their defeat at Riet and Pforte, the remainder of the *Schutztruppe's* Right Wing pulled back to points near Ebony along the *Otavibahn*. Their mission was to harass and hinder the South African advance, but their strength was not sufficient for the task. Lieutenant Venuleth continued his work using dynamite and obsolete ammunition to build and lay hundreds of mines in the passes and road crossings. The South Africans' respect for these "ungentlemanly" weapons served to slow their forward progress. The Germans now had both their aircraft operating in the area: Lieutenant Fiedler and his LFG Roland Bi-plane and Austrian Senior Lieutenant von Scheele and his Aviatik B1. Both were now providing aerial reconnaissance of Botha's dispositions and the occasional bombing of his camps. German mounted patrols established that, although the Union forces had large numbers of scouts forward, the main body had not yet begun to move forward.

Franke now reinforced this force with *Abteilung Ritter* (Detachment Ritter). Additionally, Major Bauszus' detachment, recently arrived at Johann Albrechts-Höhe from the south, was ordered to support Ritter with forces that consisted of three mounted companies and three artillery batteries. While Major Ritter operated along the rail-line, Bauszus was employed further south in the Swakop River Valley on Ritter's right.

South African machine-gun position at Trekkopje. (© Author's Collection)

First Rhodesian Regiment Maxim machine-gun detachment under Lieutenant
Hollingsworth, who was killed at Trekkopje. (© Namibian National Archives)

After a number of reconnaissance flights over Riet, Arandis, and Trekkopje, the
pilots brought back intelligence that enticed the German commander to attack Trekkopje.
Franke was keen to delay the South Africans to ensure his southern forces were able to
withdraw to the north where he now planned to group his forces for an extended campaign.
He tasked Ritter to guard the railway along the Windhoek-Karibib-Onguati line until all
the southern troops had passed to the north. Ritter's forces were concentrated between
Usakos and Stingbank east of Skinner's position.

On 22 April, Franke telegraphed Ritter an order to attack Trekkopje. Ritter's
command was augmented with one of Bauszus' companies and now consisted of five
mounted companies and two mountain-gun artillery batteries, each with four guns. Aerial
reconnaissance flights determined that the Union strength at Trekkopje was such that
a surprise attack by Ritter's force could overwhelm their defenses. Although the pilots
reported strong enemy camps further west at Arandis and Rössing, they were unable to
determine whether heavy artillery support was available.

Von Scheele again overflew the objective on the 25th and saw that the South African
strength had increased markedly to at least 1,000 men, thereby swinging the advantage
to the defender. He was forced to cut short his flight because of heavy anti-aircraft canon
fire and returned home without dropping any of his bombs. Unknown to the Germans
was the early March arrival in the territory of 12 steel-plated Rolls-Royces of the Royal
Naval Air Service (RNAS) Armored Car Division No. 1 Squadron.[44] Since 23 April, three

---

44   This was the first deployment of the cars outside Europe, pre-dating Royal Naval Air Service Armored Car
Division No 2 Squadron's deployment to the North African desert and Palestine by almost a year. The cars
were based on Henry Royce's Silver Ghost and each was protected with 9mm thick armor plate all around

sections of three of these formidable weapons were sitting at Trekkopje. Von Scheele either misreported the cars as water tankers or did not see them at all. In any event, they would provide an unwelcome greeting to Ritter's men.

Following von Scheele's flight, Ritter telephoned Franke in Windhoek to report the increased enemy presence and recommended cancelling the attack. Franke would not change his mind and ordered Ritter to proceed with the planned operation.[45]

The conditions at Trekkopje were difficult at best. The troops all suffered from the boredom inherent in guard duty. Trekkopje is a desolate place and April is extremely hot and dry in the desert. Captain F.E. Jackson, the Northern Force signal officer wrote that thermometers burst when the temperature climbed over 130 degrees Fahrenheit.[46] The strong winds across the flat ground picked up the fine sand, blasting men, animals, and machine until a coat of dust covered everything and the grit found its way into clothing, guns, and food. The camp at Kilometer 80 had been occupied since April 22nd and the only entertainment was a weekly church service and the occasional appearance of "Fritz," the German aviator who buzzed the camps and tossed the random bomb or three. That provided the troopers on the ground and the crew of "Skinny Liz" with some excitement and a spot of target practice. "Fritz," being either von Scheele or Fiedler depending on which pilot had duty, got away in each case with minor damage to the airplanes. The planes were more susceptible to mechanical failures or the difficulties of flying an underpowered machine in the hot climate than to enemy fire. Additionally, Skinner's heavy guns were pulled back to Swakopmund because no action was anticipated at Trekkopje, further disheartening the troops.

Distribution of Forces at Trekkopje
26 April 1915

German *Schutztruppe*
***Abteilung Ritter* – Major Ritter**

2nd Reserve Company – Captain Schultetus (advance guard)	
1st Company	
2nd Company – Captain von Watter	
8th Company	
9th Company	
1st Mountain-gun Battery (7.5 cm L/14 M. 08)	4 Guns
2nd Mountain-gun Battery (7.5 cm L/14 M. 08)	4 Guns
Total Strength	ca. 700 Rifles

and mounted a Vickers .303 caliber machine-gun in a rotating turret.

45　Oelhafen, p.187.

46　F.E. Jackson, quoted in Doreen Barfield, "The Battle of Trekkoppies," *Military History Journal*, Vol 2, No 2, Dec 1971.

South African & Allied Forces
3rd Infantry Brigade – General P.C.B. Skinner

2nd Transvaal Scottish Battalion	ca. 400 Rifles
2nd Kimberley Regiment	ca. 400 Rifles
1st Rhodesian Regiment – LTC (Temp) F.R. Burnside	ca. 450 Rifles
1st Imperial Light Horse (ILH), 5th Mounted Rifles	3 Squadrons
Machine-gun Sections (.303 caliber Maxim)	unknown
RNAS Armored Car Squadron Number 1	3 Sections: 9 cars
(The 4th section of three cars was in reserve at Arandis)	
1 x BLC 15-pdr Armstrong Anti-Aircraft Gun "Skinny Liz"	1 Gun
Total Strength	ca. 1,300 Rifles
In Reserve at Swakopmund:	
Heavy Artillery Battery (12 pdr 18 cwt guns)	2 Guns
Heavy Artillery Section (4.7 inch QF guns)	2 Guns

On the night of 25/26 April, Skinner left his deputy Lieutenant Colonel TH Rodgers in command and headed north to scout along the railway line towards Ebony with a squadron of the Imperial Light Horse. Meanwhile, the Germans were advancing towards Trekkopje.

Further to the south, Major Bauszus was tasked to carry out a diversion towards Riet down the Swakop River Valley and was moving west with his mounted companies while Ritter moved 44 kilometers along the rail-line from Usakos with five companies and two mountain-gun batteries, a column of nearly 1,000 men and animals. Ritter planned to turn west about five kilometers north of Trekkopje and use a ridgeline that paralleled the rail to cover his advance. He would return through a pass that had already been reconnoitered towards the railway and attack the camp directly in its left flank while the eight mountain-guns covered the assault. At the same time, a party of engineers was to attack the railway line south of Trekkopje to cut off the camp from any reinforcements that might come from Arandis. A good plan in essence, but as Thucydides observed, many things are unpredictable in war and outcomes are never certain.

As Ritter and his forces marched south, Skinner and his band were moving north. Two ships in the night as it were, but early in the morning Skinner's advance scouts observed Ritter's forces who were unaware their presence had been discovered.[47] Skinner turned his element around and rode with all haste back to Trekkopje to raise the alarm and ordered the 1st Rhodesian Regiment forward to reinforce the position. The Imperial Light Horse (ILH) was positioned on the right flank where the commander expected the German attack to concentrate.

At Trekkopje, defensive trench of the Kimberley Regiment stretched west from a small culvert in the rail-line then arched to the rear for about 500 meters. The Kimberleys also had a number of .303 caliber Maxim machine-guns positioned along their line. The

---

47   L'Ange quotes one story that a German officer ordered Skinner's troops to get into the proper march position as they passed; it is more likely is that Skinner's advance guard saw the Germans and were able to report back to him without being observed by their opponents.

Transvaal Scottish were in position perpendicular to the rail on the east side of the railway, forward of the station building. "Skinny Liz" was in position close to the station at the rail along with two of the armored cars. Five more cars were behind the main line and two were held in reserve further to the rear. Behind the lines, south-west of the station were three rows of bell tents that would soon provide the German gunners a good aiming point. The Rhodesians arrived ten minutes before the first artillery round fell and were initially positioned behind the Union regiments near the railway station.

Ritter had turned behind the ridge and Skinner's advanced guard lost contact with the Germans when they disappeared. Ritter's march continued until he reached what he believed was the correct pass and turned back towards the railway. He suddenly realized he misjudged his location and was about five kilometers directly in front of the Union forces requiring his forces to advance over open ground.

Just before early morning light, the German engineers detonated two charges, but they also misjudged their position and destroyed the railway on the wrong side of the camp, north at Kilometer 82, instead of south between Arandis and the camp. Ritter's artillery barrage began at 0700 from 4,300 meters; the first of about 300 shells started to fall on the Union camp. The amply forewarned Union forces were protected in their defensive positions rather than their tents, but could only wait for the storm of steel to stop. After the action, one South African wrote that he would never again disparage the German's shooting abilities.[48] The *Schutztruppe* rode under the cover of the artillery fire to close within a kilometer of the camp before beginning a dismounted attack focused on the Union center at the railway. With the heavy artillery fire shredding many of the tents, the Germans closed to within 500 meters. The ILH attempted to flank the Germans from the east side, but heavy rifle and artillery fire dissuaded the attempt and they backed off. Ritter shifted the first then the second artillery battery forward to about 1,500 meters from the Union forces to better support the infantry, while the attack shifted towards the center of the Union line. Heavy fire from Lieutenants Kidd and Hollingsworth's Maxims, and the seven Vickers of the armored cars blunted the assault and forced the Germans to shift the attack to the Union left. Ritter committed his last company around 0800 but again the assault faltered. The artillery batteries were also running low on ammunition. The Rhodesians had shifted position to reinforce the left wing and were pressuring Ritter's western flank, while the ILH rode out on the far eastern side, harassing the Germans with long-range rifle fire. The armored cars remained relatively unscathed as they roamed back and forth firing their guns behind the protected railway embankment.

Between 0900 and 1000, Captain Schultetus reported dust clouds on the horizon approaching the battleground. Anticipating an enemy counterattack, Ritter called off the attack and ordered a phased withdrawal. The companies broke off the engagement and pulled back in good order towards Stingbank while the artillery covered their withdrawal. The 1st Mountain-gun battery provided extended, accurate covering fire, itself protected by the 8th Company as the Germans assembled and marched off to the north. "Skinny Liz" managed to fire one round at the departing Germans. Contrary to official accounts, Skinner did not mount a counterattack and the armored cars that could have chased the Germans remained in camp.[49]

---

48   Left Arm, "The Action at Trekkopje – A Day of Lost Opportunities for the PBI in South West Africa", *Springbok*. Author's note: PBI means "poor bloody infantry."
49   Ibid.

The Germans left 11 dead on the battlefield while the Union forces lost nine troopers, one of them Lieutenant Hollingsworth, the last Rhodesian to be killed in the campaign. The German 2nd Company commander Captain Freiherr von Watter was killed during the withdrawal as the last man to leave the battlefield. He was found pistol in hand fighting to the last. Accounts from both sides attest to the respect each held for the bravery, skill, and resilience of their opponents. This would be the last engagement of the Swakop River Valley campaign save the escape from Otjimbingwe of one of Bauszus' companies in three day's time. It was the beginning of the end.

6

"The End is Near"

Otjimbingwe

Immediately after Trekkopje, Botha began the next phase of his advance. His build-up of supplies at Riet was complete and he had two additional mounted brigades, each with an attached field artillery battery. The General planned to concentrate his forces on Karibib were he suspected the main body of the German forces were located. At the same time, he sent two UDF brigades towards Kubas and Otjimbingwe to secure that line of march in case the Germans were lying directly east between Riet and Windhoek. In actuality, only the *Schutztruppe* 3rd Company was in front of the Union forces. The company was located 70 kilometers south of Karibib at Kaltenhausen in an advance guard position. On 29 April, alerted of the South Africans' approach, the company pulled back to Otjimbingwe, where it thought it could stand down for a day. The commander failed to post adequate security, which allowed the *Burgher* to encircle the town. In the ensuing melee, the South Africans failed to close the door completely and the 3rd Company escaped through the gap, sacrificing one platoon to cover their withdrawal. The platoon was captured and the prisoners added to the South Africans' growing list of POWs. For their part, the Germans were keeping South African POWs in locations near Tsumeb having moved them north before the Baster revolt.

Governor von Seitz shifted his capital to Grootfontein in the north and Franke decided to concentrate his forces near Otavi and Waterberg. Key to Franke's withdrawal plan was the rail terminus at Onguati that lay 13 kilometers northwest of Karibib. Windhoek was to be abandoned as it was militarily indefensible and unnecessary to Franke's overall strategy. The *Schutztruppe's* remaining supplies would be moved by rail from Windhoek, through Okahandja, then west towards Karibib and Onguati. There the line turned north towards Otavi and the copper mining region. If Botha moved too quickly, however, the railway would be cut and Franke's plan frustrated. As it was, the last load passed Onguati before Botha's troops arrived. All they managed to capture was an empty train.

Von Kleist's forces moved north from Rehoboth by train and then off-loaded at Okahandja to continue the march on horse to Waterberg on 4 May. Major Ritter and his detachment set about destroying the bridges after the final train passed on their way up the rail line, while Bauszus headed north further inland.

Botha and his juggernaut kept marching and by 5 May, occupied Karibib. By the 12th, they took Windhoek, which also had been abandoned. Only the 4th Replacement Company failed to move north because it had lost all its horses. The vanguard of Botha's mounted column discovered the company east of town and following a short fire-fight, the soldiers were forced to capitulate. The only other elements still in the south were the 7th Camel Company, the 3rd Company, and Captain Graf von Saurma-Jeltsch's detachment that had been engaged with the Baster uprising. The 7th and 3rd Companies moved overland arriving near Waterberg at the end of May. Now only Saurma-Jeltsch's element remained. Arriving in Rehoboth on 11 May, they proceeded by train to a point 40 kilometers south of Windhoek, offloaded, and marched east to skirt the city, to avoid meeting the UDF they knew to be approaching the capital. They would reach the Waterberg on 2 June, the last element to arrive in the north.

Botha now held a line from Swakopmund to Windhoek and as far north as Okahandja. The railway had been rebuilt as far as Ebony and soon would be finished to Karibib. From there Botha planned to use the existing German *Otavibahn* to follow Franke up country. When rail service was re-established to Windhoek, the South Africans were moving up to 200 tons of supplies per day to supply the advance.[1] To move the supplies from Cape Town, four warships and 27 freighters, including many confiscated German ships of the Woermann and East Africa Lines, were in service. The terrain had also changed. The central plateau region was not as forbidding as the harsh gravel plains and sand dunes of the coastal region. The empty desert gave way to brush and various varieties of acacia, including the camel thorn with its formidable barbs that tore at man and animal alike. Despite the change in terrain, water was still scarce and remained a critical logistical problem for the UDF and Germans alike.

Morale in the *Schutztruppe* plummeted with the loss of Windhoek, as much for the loss of the capital as for the capture of the radio station, which had provided news of German victories in Europe. A saying made its way through the German ranks that pinned all hope on the larger war to the north: "The future of the colonies will be forged on the battlefields of Europe."

Meanwhile, Franke received information that not just native guides, but some Germans had quit the fight and were now aiding Botha. A former policeman and volunteer soldier named "Witwer" went over to the Union forces and led them into Otjimbingwe where the 3rd Company was surrounded and nearly overwhelmed. He then guided them to Wilhelmstal.[2] Other deserters were reported to be assisting Botha on the route north towards Waterberg.

From his new command post at Omaruru, Franke ordered the local commander, Captain Rothmaler, to survey a defensive position near Khorab at Kilometer 514 on the railway, about 15 kilometers north of Otavi, and ordered the magazine at Grootfontein to be shifted to Tsumeb and then to Namutoni. Franke planned to withdraw north into Ovamboland.

The Final Chase

Franke summed up his assessment of an already clear situation in an early June 1915 diary entry, stating, "The end is in the near future."[3] He was speaking only of the situation in the colony, as the news coming from Europe was positive. Germany held the advantage and stood before the gates of Paris. *Schutztruppe* officers and soldiers shared the news and rumors alike. Most of all they hoped a victory on the battlefields of Europe would preserve the colony. Three more years would have to pass before the colonies' ultimate fate would be known, although the war in GSWA would end sooner.

In late May, Governor von Seitz sent a proposal to General Botha for a meeting to discuss "terms". On 20 May, an armistice was declared and von Seitz and Botha met at

---

1   These shipments were extremely labor intensive as the cargos had to be unloaded and reloaded at every destroyed bridge or when the railway gauge required a train change.
2   Victor Franke, *Tagebuch: 1896-1920*, p.981.
3   Franke, p.983.

South African Captain Richter of the Imperial Light Horse going out under white flag at Karibib for negotiations at Giftkuppe on May 20 1915. (© Namibian National Archives)

Giftkuppe, a site equidistant from Omaruru and Karibib. Botha assented to the meeting and arrived at the site the next day by motorcar, while von Seitz and the German delegation came south by train. The negotiations were destined to fail, as von Seitz's proposal to end hostilities would have left all territory above the 22nd parallel in German hands. Botha probably suspected the Germans were bluffing and insisted on unconditional surrender, which von Seitz turned down. The meeting ended without results and the cease-fire was lifted the following day.

Botha now planned for his final gambit with five mounted brigades of 13,000 troops and 20,000 animals. The General could also count on five batteries of QF 13-pdr guns plus four sections of heavy artillery. Their opponents in front of them comprised nine active and eight reserve mounted companies, three dismounted companies, and nine artillery batteries.[4] The *Schutztruppe*'s total front-line manpower by this time was around 3,000 personnel, many of whom were untrained fire department, postal and administrative service personnel.

Botha's objective would be the suspected German concentration at Tsumeb and he would use his favorite tactic, *izimpondo zankomo*, to ensnare the Germans once and for all.[5] Colonel Brits' 1st Brigade was to move north to Omaruru and then east along the Etosha Pan to Namutoni to be on the left wing. Colonel Myburgh commanding the 2nd and 3rd Brigades would proceed east close to the Waterberg to Grootfontein and then swing around the right side of Tsumeb, while Lukin, along with Brigadiers P.S. Beves and H.W.M.

---

4   More precisely, Franke had at his disposal three mountain-gun batteries and three FK 96 n/A batteries, while two batteries had the older, obsolete FK 96 a/A guns. One of the batteries had no limbers or horses and another was a three-gun anti-aircraft battery.

5   Meaning in Zulu: the horns of the beast – the classic tactic of double envelopment employing a center force to fix the enemy and two elements or "horns" that encircled his flanks.

Captured German 7.7cm Model 96 a/A artillery pieces on railcars ready to be transported to South Africa after the surrender. These are the same type guns used by *Freikorps* inside South Africa during the Boer Rebellion. (© Namibian National Archives)

"Mannie" Botha would canter straight up the middle with the bulk of the forces, the 5th and 6th Mounted Brigades and the 1st Infantry Brigade, with a total of twelve 13-pdrs and six heavy artillery pieces. Lukin would be the fixing force, while Brits and Myburgh would encircle the Germans to prevent their escape and destroy them if necessary. The UDF's new air force was in full operation during June. The Henri Farman airplanes would prove especially valuable to pinpoint major German positions thoughout the rest of the campaign.

In a nod to his Herero antagonists of the 1904-1908 uprisings, Franke briefly attempted to conduct irregular bush warfare (*Kleinkrieg*) on a limited basis in the rear areas of the South African forces. Almost half-heartedly, he dispatched *Busch Patrouille*, small mounted detachments, to harass and delay Botha. His order was simple: "Stop the enemy, attack where possible!" The patrols had no clear objective, however, and operated more like independent combat reconnaissance teams that engaged the South Africans wherever and whenever they found them. Sabotaging the railway was one objective; the independent 7th Camel Company was able to demolish tracks near Ebony, while other patrols destroyed tracks and bridges between Windhoek and Okahandja. All of these operations took place deep inside UDF-controlled territory, but the cost to the Germans was often more dear than the temporary disruptions they accomplished. Many of these patrols went out and simply did not return. South African scouts were operating in force forward of the main body and, if they were encountered, the almost always smaller German patrols usually had to fight their way out or were captured. One patrol managed to evade capture for over two weeks and then stumbled, disoriented, half-starved and thirsty into a South African base where they were taken prisoner. Herero and Damara bandits were also roaming the countryside and proved dangerous, as the patrols were lucrative targets. Ambushes cost the Germans a number of irreplaceable men and valuable mounts, not to mention rifles. The effort was likened to "many dozens of mosquito bites, but ineffective against an enemy that flooded the territory".[6]

Nonetheless, the patrols provided intelligence that gave Franke an idea of Botha's intentions, but it was an incomplete picture. For several days Brits' forces were able to move north without being detected. It was only when a German farmer told a *Schutztruppe* patrol of the UDF presence to the west near the Etosha Pan that Franke realized a double envelopment was in progress.

Franke knew he had little time, but he had not expected the South Africans to move as fast as they did and his plan to prepare defenses near Kilometer 514 had a critical weakness – the South Africans did not have to attack the position to defeat the Germans, they could just wait the Germans out.

It suddenly became clear to the Germans that a defense of the waterholes near Otavifontein, south of Tsumeb, would be necessary. With the understanding that Botha wished to encircle their forces, the Germans now assessed that the South African main force would converge at Otavifontein and await the pincers of Brits and Myburgh to complete the trap. If Botha would not attack it, the original defensive position at Kilometer 514 would be useless.

Franke had already begun to contemplate capitulation, but Governor von Seitz first wanted a victory of some sort on which to base negotiated terms. Von Seitz believed he would be subject to repercussions if he surrendered the protectorate. Franke wrote in late June that the Governor was complaining about his military leadership and that all responsibility for failure would lie on his own shoulders.

Franke gave Ritter the mission to defend Otavifontein, but despite the strong position he occupied, the defense would fail.[7] Ritter did not have time to build up his defenses and many of the advance posts were not occupied as the South Africans approached.

When the South African main force of Lukin and Mannie Botha struck on 1 July 1915, the German forces conducted a fighting withdrawal and abandoned the critical water source to their opponent after five hours of battle. Had the Germans been able to mount an effective defense, the UDF would have been forced to return south as no other water was available to them. This would have given Franke several weeks to determine his next move. Now, however, Botha was in a comfortable position to wait for the encirclement to be completed. Beves and the dismounted 1st Infantry Brigade would arrive on July 6th after a 13-day, 230-mile march from the south.

The Germans were by this time conditioned to retreat. Indeed, Franke lamented in his diary that his subordinate officers often pulled back in the face of the enemy's advance and offered no resistance to delay them. More likely than not, this was a trait picked up from their commander's own hesitance to engage the enemy. Many of the German officers and men had lost confidence in Franke's ability to command and his own demeanor, coupled with the last minute decision to fortify Otavifontein, probably reinforced this doubt about

6   Richard Hennig, *Deutsch-Südwest im Weltkrieg*, p.228.
7   Both Collyer and Hennig believed the Germans had the advantage of a strong position at Otavifontein, but were forced out by the speed of the South African advance and the lack of time to prepare defensive positions. Collyer and L'Ange thought the Germans had an advantage in artillery, but that was in numbers only as most of the German guns were obsolete, some dating from the 1880s, and they were served by inexperienced or untrained crews. The official German history states the 800 defenders of Otavifontein were opposed by 7-8,000 UDF troops, while Collyer states about 3,700 UDF troops were present. Nevertheless, another opportunity for the Germans was lost.

his competence.

The South Africans were fully spent after days on the march, so they halted and sat back on the waterholes to recover after the battle. To their amusement, Franke's order for the defense of the north was found on the field at Otavifontein. In it, he exhorted the German troops on to glory and described how his soldiers had thus far delayed the strong forces opposing them and caused enormous expenditure to the South Africans. J.J. Collyer caustically commented on Franke's claim, saying delays and costs were incurred not as a result of German effort, but solely due to internal problems of the South African forces.[8]

By 1 July, Brits had nearly reached Namutoni, while Myburgh had captured Grootfontein and was proceeding north-west to flank the Germans on their east side.

The Germans were now faced with a decision to surrender or fight on. Although a number of soldiers and officers considered carrying on the fight, Franke and the majority of his senior officers felt it would be useless to continue. Retreating across the Angolan border was briefly discussed, but the objective would have been to turn themselves over to the Portuguese for internment, not to fight on. The idea of carrying on a guerrilla war was rejected as too difficult under the conditions; it would also have subjected the German settlers and POWs to retribution from the occupying South Africans. The Germans considered Ovamboland as hostile territory, both because of the war-like peoples who inhabited it and the difficulties of living in the region, which was malarial and had little available food suitable for the force. They also rejected a plan to defend the position at Kilometer 514 as a fortress, fully expecting the South Africans would simply refuse to attack and leave the defenders to starve. Governor von Seitz reluctantly agreed with the plan to negotiate surrender. A note to that effect was sent to Botha on 3 July.

On 4 July, another debacle shook the Germans. Franke had posted Captain von Kleist at Grootfontein to protect his flank, perhaps assuming von Kleist had learned from his near disaster at Gibeon. He had not. After falling back on Ghaub with the approach of Myburgh before Grootfontein, von Kleist again failed to place adequate advance guards in the direction of the enemy. Although a large dust cloud was seen on the horizon, von Kleist did not send out a reconnaissance to determine its source nor were the troops alerted to prepare for an attack. The small German force was surprised and, once again, forced to fight their way out of near encirclement. Falling back, von Kleist and his unit joined with on the main force at Khorab. Myburgh continued on and closed the door at Tsumeb – only a small sliver of space was available for an escape. That space closed on July 5th as Brits' advance eliminated the last available escape route to the northwest.

Meeting at Kilometer 500 on the *Otavibahn*, the protagonists argued over the surrender documents, but few changes to Botha's stipulations were made. The negotiations did not go as the Germans wished; Botha held to the same demand for an unconditional surrender that he made at Giftkuppe. On 9 July 1915, the surrender documents were signed by General Botha and Governor von Seitz and took immediate effect. The Germans would be allowed to keep their weapons, officers their pistols, active troopers their rifles without ammunition, and reservists would be sent home with rifles and a limited supply of cartridges for protection. Active soldiers and non-commissioned officers were to be interned, while the officers would have freedom of movement within the colony as long as they pledged not to fight again. The Austrian pilot, Lieutenant Fielder, refused and was interned. Mine

---

8   J.J. Collyer, *The Campaign in German South West Africa*, p.159.

German *Schutztruppe* prisoners at the South African POW camp near Aus
in southern SWA after the capitulation in July 1915. The Germans were
held here under UDF until 1919. (© Namibian National Archives)

specialist Lieutenant Venuleth agreed and days later he told Franke that he was working
with the victors to locate and disarm all his mines. General Botha and his South African
army had conquered German South West Africa.

Observations on the Campaign

With the end of the campaign, the South Africans deservedly celebrated a relatively
quick and easy victory. General Botha had recovered an army's pride that had been lost
at Sandfontein. In the South West African (SWA) campaign, the South Africans had
learned a number of valuable lessons, not all of which served them in their next endeavor.
The "Springboks" would move on to more difficult battlefields, German East Africa (GEA),
where they would be severely tested over the next three years against a German commander
who understood how to defend as well as attack in the face of a much larger force, and at
Delville Wood in Europe.

The problems of an inadequate and inexperienced staff and the lack of advance
planning bedeviled the UDF in East Africa as much as it did during their first deployment.
The difficulty of logistics and providing adequate supplies there would be magnified several
times over what they experienced in SWA, as the distances were longer, the terrain more
difficult, and the environment often harsher. Moreover, tropical disease would cost both
sides greatly there. Tactically, the commanders had learned how important communication
was for effective operations. But their opponent in East Africa had a different kind of
commander as well.

Understanding that a post-mortem critique always benefits from hindsight, it is still possible to take issue with a number of decisions that accelerated the German defeat in SWA. A general observation is necessary: the Germans in SWA had begun the war with an overwhelming expectation of probable defeat.

Heydebreck correctly prioritized the defense of the south first, which paid off with a victory at Sandfontein, but Franke did not make contingency plans for any other scenario until it was too late to confront the South Africans in the north with any chance of success.

Nor were all of Heydebreck's decisions sound. His decision not to contest the South African landing at Lüderitzbucht (as with Franke later at Swakopmund) has often been criticized. Colonel von Lettow-Vorbeck's success against General Aitken's Indian Expeditionary Force "B" landing at Tanga in German East Africa is often cited as an example of what a spirited defense could have accomplished.[9] In GSWA, the defenders believed the guns of the Royal Navy ships were too much of a threat to challenge the landing.[10] Had the Germans attacked when the South Africans were in the process of landing, the navy would have been hard pressed to provide supporting fire given the proximity of the combatants to each other. Although the outcome of challenges to the landings might be debatable, those were the last times the forces stood, if only briefly, on relatively equal terms. The German expectation that they would be able to accomplish much more inland permitted the South Africans to gain vital coastal foot-holds on the two most important ports in the territory and effectively cut-off any hope of outside assistance. Furthermore, because the Germans did not confront the South Africans at Lüderitzbucht or on the border, Botha and Smuts were able to deal with an internal rebellion with little concern for their enemy to the north – at least until they resumed operations in GSWA.

Additionally, when Heydebreck ordered Major Franke's punitive expedition against Portuguese Angola in October 1914, he diverted much-needed resources for nearly three months and sapped the energy of troops and animals that could have been better employed elsewhere.

Franke's conduct of the war also left much to be desired and, although his colleagues ascribe to him great courage as the "Hero of Omaruru", his leadership as commander of the *Schutztruppe* was not of the same caliber. Most importantly, Franke, in holding on to Heydebreck's strategy, looked more to evasion, rather than confrontation. In so doing, he placed his emphasis on conserving his force and concentrated on retreat rather than enagement. Further, once he assumed command, he seemed to lack confidence in his own abilities. Franke's diary and the official German report of the war reflect that he was weighed down by these anxieties. Moreover, von Oelhafen claimed that Franke had lost the confidence of his men.[11]

The *Schutztruppe* was never intended to be anything more than a "protection force" to provide internal security for the protectorate, nor was it given the resources for war on

---

9   Although chance and luck were on von Lettow-Vorbeck's side at Tanga, the quick reorganization of his defenses ensured the Allied landing was a failure.

10   As in East Africa, the Germans were following instructions from the Colonial Office not to oppose the landings. Like von Lettow-Vorbeck at Tanga, Heydebreck could have chosen to ignore those instructions.

11   Franke was probably also addicted to morphine, which could have contributed to his behavior. Dr Karl-Heinz Minuth, the transcriber of Franke's diary, believed Franke referred to his need for the drug using the abbreviation 'MS' (*Morphinsulfat*) on numerous occasions in the text. South African intelligence biographic sketches of Franke gave similar indications. See Ian Van der Waag, "The battle of Sandfontein, 26 September 1914: South African military, reform and the German South-West Africa campaign, 1914–1915, *First World War Studies*, DOI: 10.1080/19475020.2013.828633.

a European scale. The same could be said of GEA, where von Lettow-Vorbeck led a force made up of a small number of white officers and non-commissioned officers with the bulk of the force being native *Askari*. Whereas von Lettow-Vorbeck had nearly two years to prepare his troops before the British invaded on a large scale, Heydebreck had just months. Similar to the decision in GSWA not to confront a British landing, the Germans in East Africa initially withdrew from the coast. Here the Governor was the driving force behind this, however, not the military commander who disagreed with the decision.

There were significant differences between German East and South West Africa. First, there were fewer Germans in East Africa, roughly 5,000 or half the population of GSWA. At the outset of the war, the *Schutztruppe* in GEA numbered just over 200 Germans and 2,500 *Askari*. These numbers would climb to 1,600 and 12,000 respectively at the force's maximum strength in 1916.[12] And, although the Germans did not oppose the British at Dar es Salam, they were there to meet them and turn back the landings at Tanga. They also invaded British territory and occupied it – if only temporarily. The Germans in East Africa also possessed less modern equipment; the *Askari* were mostly armed with the obsolete M1871 rifle with its smoky, black powder cartridge that significantly disadvantaged the rifleman by pinpointing his position to the enemy. This would change as resupply by German blockade-runners and battlefield captures permitted the *Askari* to be equipped with modern rifles. Nevertheless, von Lettow-Vorbeck was able to carry out a mobile defense that successfully wore down and delayed Allied efforts to capture the territory through the end of the war.

In GSWA, the fear of a native uprising precluded any consideration of arming and training the natives. The military and civilian leadership had little confidence in their ability to lead or control a military made up of indigenous troops, while the other German colonies made good use of native troops. Nowhere was this better evidenced than in East Africa.

Franke also rejected fighting a *Kleinkrieg* or bush war. The official report of the war evaluated the idea and found it improbable that the *Schutztruppe* could have carried on for much longer. It argued the *Schutztruppe* in GSWA lacked the training to fight as guerrillas in the bush for an extended period.[13] Additionally, the lack of potable water, suitable forage, and the health of the men and their mounts in a hostile environment were cited as negative factors. In 1915, the northern areas of Ovamboland and the Omaheke were in what was then known as the "starving time" – a severe drought that had hit the native population hard. Under such conditions, it was thought doubtful the Germans troops could have long endured.

Intelligence operations also played a role in the German defeat. With the exception of the Battle of Sandfontein, the South Africans took every opportunity to employ intelligence assets and use the information gained from them to conduct operations.[14]

---

12 GEA Governor Schnee reported that von Lettow-Vorbeck's army numbered 155 Germans, 1,168 askari, along with 2,000 porters at its surrender in November 1918 at Abercorn, Northern Rhodesia.

13 This is debatable. When properly employed, the *Schutztruppe* showed great skill in small unit reconnaissance and combat operations, whereas their ability to coordinate and conduct large, combined operations was limited. Much depended on the capabilities of the individual unit commanders.

14 The Germans had deployed advance scouts and surveillance elements and were possibly aided by a South African traitor that revealed the attack plan. The Germans not only located and tracked the South Africans, but also repelled a UDF relief column, ensuring the failure of the UDF plan. It would be one of the last such intelligence successes the Germans would pull off during the campaign. See Ian Van der

As General Botha moved forward from Walvis Bay, he deployed the UDF's intelligence units, to reconnoitre the territory in advance of the front line while using signal units to monitor German wireless transmissions. The combination of both methods allowed Botha to accurately determine the placement and strength of his opponent while the Germans remained largely in the dark about what was to their front.

Botha was able to estimate the enemy strength and disposition – including commanders' names – with some accuracy. A report by Major J.G.W. Leipoldt, DSO, a surveyor and intelligence officer with Botha's General Headquarters, shows the detail the South Africans had garnered from intercepts:

> The Pforte position was known to be occupied by at least 2 mounted companies (German company 175 to 200 rifles) and a section of Field Artillery. The Riet position by at least four mounted companies and a battery of Field Artillery, while a general reserve of two batteries and four or five companies was at Jackalswater and Modderfontein.[15]

Despite knowing the precise location of Botha's camp at Husab, the Germans were unaware of his advance until a forward outpost was engaged by a UDF advance element not far from their position at Pforte on March 19th. Compounding the losses at Pforte, the documents abandoned at Modderfontein allowed General Botha to concentrate his forces to pursue and eventually conduct an encirclement that would force the German surrender.

As they moved forward, the South Africans also aggressively sought out informants among the local population who provided reports on the strength of the German forces, as well as defensive measures such as land mine and booby trap emplacements.[16] The Germans, given their negative history with the indigenous peoples of GSWA, had no counter to the South African tactics.

With the arrival of the new South African Aviation Corps in the spring of 1915, Botha was able to exploit aerial reconnaissance to locate the Germans and coordinate operations between his own columns. While the Germans were the first to employ aircraft in the theatre, at Trekkopje Franke failed to heed the intelligence they provided.

In the final analysis and although the Germans were greatly outnumbered, their failure to properly use intelligence assets such as reconnaissance forces or correct wireless procedures they knew to be poor much hastened their defeat.

It is easy to compare the circumstances in GSWA to those von Lettow-Vorbeck's troops endured in East Africa, but there were other differences. In GEA, the commander had prepared for the eventuality of a small war nearly from the outset of the campaign. After initially attempting to fight a more conventional, but mobile campaign, he adapted

---

Waag, op.cit.

15   Major JGW Leipoldt, DSO, report on operations in German South West Africa submitted to the War Office by the South African Government, available at http://www.kaiserscross.com/41992/home.html. Leipoldt was appointed as Captain in the South African Permanent Force , one of the first 51 officers commissioned in July 1912. He would be instrumental in forming the Intelligence Sub-Branch in the UDF Headquarters in late 1917. See also: Major I.J. van der Waag, "Major J.G.W. Leipoldt, DSO: A Portrait of a South African Surveyor and Intelligence Officer, 1912-1923," *Scientia Militaria*, Vol 25, No 1, 1995, pp.12-34.

16   Collyer, op.cit. The UDF experience with guides was spotty. On at least two occasions, commanders had to relieve their guides and navigate by compass and dead reckoning because their advance had gone astray.

his methods and organization to a different form of warfare: "guerrilla war." It was a change that was influenced by his experiences in GSWA during the native uprisings.[17] He concentrated on logistics and set up artisanal factories to manufacture quinine to combat malaria, while others made synthetic fuel for vehicles. There were also German farms that provided food for the troops. What they needed, they captured from their opponents.[18] The *Schutztruppe* in GEA were also marching on foot with hundreds of porters to carry supplies and the native troops were better accustomed to foraging for their own needs. Franke, on the other hand, was not mentally prepared to carry out *Kleinkrieg* nor had he prepared his forces for that eventuality. Knowing he was outnumbered, he seemed resigned to surrender rather than commit to resistance.

The outcome of the campaign was probably inevitable no matter what course the Germans chose. Different decisions might have delayed the South Africans, as happened in East Africa, but, most importantly, the mindset to take those steps did not exist in *Südwest*. The failures that ultimately brought the Germans to capitulate were failures of command.

The battles in the Swakop River Valley and at Gibeon were the last major confrontations between Union and German forces in GSWA. The German decision to abandon the field with little resistance after these battles left the corridor into the country open to a rapid UDF advance and victory.

On 9 July 1915, about 4,400 *Schutztruppe* officers and other ranks surrendered to South African forces. That number included both active service and reserve troops, of which 1,900 were front line combat troops.

---

17 Hew Strachan, in his book *The First World War in Africa*, disputes the use of the term "guerrilla warfare" to describe von Lettow-Vorbeck's methods as he considers the necessary component of "national liberation" to be lacking. As the German term *Kleinkrieg* (small war) has the same meaning as the Spanish word "guerrilla", Strachan's argument is specious. Clearly, the Germans executed a successful mobile defense of an irregular nature against a much larger force, a war that was dispersed over large expanses of the territory.

18 Although a few blockade running ships succeeded in bringing arms and ammunition to GEA.

7

The Battlefields Today

The campaign that was fought in the Swakop River Valley and up the central highlands of South West Africa covered around 800 kilometers of difficult terrain. For the German and South African troops who made the trek from the south, the distance covered was nearly 1,600 kilometers. The skirmishes and major engagements took place at locations that are, for the most part, widely separated with the exception of the battles described herein. In an area not more than 60 kilometers across, four major and a number of minor engagements took place in the space of 60 days, but none of these sites have yet been preserved.

The sites at Husab, Riet, Pforte, Jakalswater and Trekkopje all contain evidence of the battles – from artifacts strewn across the surface to rock "sangar" fighting positions – which have lain undisturbed for nearly 100 years.[1] The Trekkopje railway station sign, although not original, marks the site of the battle that took place there. A small war cemetery is located about 100 meters away where South African, Rhodesian, and German dead lie side by side. The old *Staatsbahn* railway is long gone. Ranchers and farmers long ago cannibalized the rails, sleepers, and most of the station buildings to recycle the wood and metal into fence lines and homes. Only the elevated railway bed remains showing the way across a desolate plain and occasionally winding through the rocky hills of the Namib.

The few other major battlefield sites in Namibia lie on private land (Sandfontein) or in areas that have been built up (Gibeon) and the traces of battle have disappeared. The Swakop River Valley campaign sites are an exception. Husab, Riet, and Pforte lie within the Namib National Park, while Jakalswater is located on a private farm; fortuitously the current owner is concerned about the site's preservation. Even though these sites are within the park boundaries, they are still threatened by progress. The *Otavibahn* rail line has been rebuilt at least two times and will soon go through a third renovation, which has disturbed much of the Trekkopje site. Additionally, the Erongo Region in which they are located is one the richest sources of uranium in the world and several companies are beginning new mining operations there. The battlefields lie close to, or within, the mining concessions and may be lost if the government takes no action to preserve the area.

Unfortunately, there is no urgency or compelling reason for anyone to care. As mentioned in the prologue, neither the current Namibian nor South African governments consider the war or the sites to be of great significance to their historical heritage. Germany has little influence with the Namibian leadership because of its colonial history and seemingly has little interest in preserving the battlefields of this forgotten campaign. Unless some action is taken, the sites will soon disappear.

The *Namib Battlefield Heritage Project: 1915-2015*, a small team working under the auspices of the *Namib Desert Archaeological Survey,* is conducting surveys to record the Swakop River Valley sites in the hopes that the Namibian Heritage Council will choose

---

1   Sangar is a British Army term used to describe a temporary fighting position made of rock, sandbags, or other protective materials and originates from the Persian word *Sang* meaning rock.

to preserve and memorialize these important historical heritage battlefields.[2] Only time will tell.

A view of Eisenbahn Pforte from the northern ridge looking to the southwest. The trace of the old *Staatsbahn* railway is visible in the center of the pass and along the western side of the ridge. (© James Stejskal)

---

2   John Kinahan and James Stejskal, "Finding Europe's Great War in Africa," *Current World Archaeology*, pp.48-51.

UDF trash dump in the center of Husab Camp. At various times during the campaign up 20,000 troopers and their animals occupied this camp. Remnants of bully beef, condensed milk, jam, and canned fish tins, along with other artifacts, still lie on the surface after 100 years. (© James Stejskal)

Remains of a UDF sangar on the eastern edge of the Husab Camp. These defensive fighting positions ringed the camp in all directions. In the background is the Swakop River Valley and the Husab and Pforte mountain chains. (© James Stejskal)

A line of German *Schutzengraben* extends southwest at the base of Langer Heinrich Mountain. (© James Stejskal)

View of Riet battlefield looking east from a hilltop near the point where the UDF held its line at mid-day. (© James Stejskal)

Aerial view of Jakalswater Station ruins looking south. The Walfischrucken
lie directly behind the buildings. At the top of the picture is the Swakop
River Valley and Riet battlefield at center. (© James Stejskal)

Ruins of Jakalswater Station viewed from the south from
the top of Walfischrucken. (© James Stejskal)

Trace of the *Staatsbahn* rail line at Jakalswater Station looking north. (© James Stejskal)

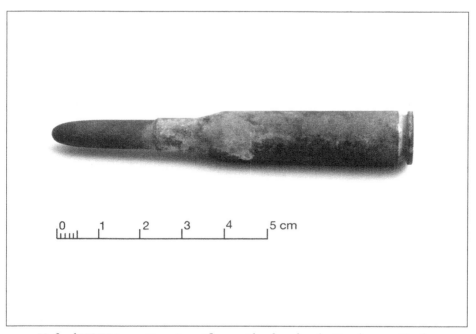

Unfired UDF Mauser-Verguiero rifle cartridge found at the Husab camp. Similar expended cartridges were found atop the Walfischrucken and on the outskirts of Jakalswater Station that confirmed UDF firing positions. (© James Stejskal)

Schutztruppe Mauser rifle cartridges found at Jakalswater Station. (© James Stejskal)

German *Schutztruppe* graves at Trekkopje. UDF and Rhodesian
graves are located nearby. (© James Stejskal)

A lone UDF grave marker located at Riet. While most of the cemeteries in the country are like those shown on the previous page, this is one of the few monuments erected by soldiers during the campaign. Lt Uys was exhumed and taken home to South Africa to be buried near his home after the war. This marker stone replaced the original sometime early in the 20th Century. (© James Stejskal)

Ruins of a building at the Aus POW camp in southern Namibia. Little remains of the camp except eroded bricks, tins, and a tended cemetery that holds South African and German soldiers alike, most of whom perished in the Influenza Pandemic of 1918. (© James Stejskal)

8

The Legacy

On 11 July 1915, the former territory of GSWA was designated the South West African Protectorate. A governor appointed by the South African Minister of Defense would be responsible for administering the territory and was authorized "to take all measures, and by proclamation to make such laws, and enforce the same, as you may deem necessary for the peace, order and good government."[1]

With those words a new era began.

At the conclusion of World War I, the Treaty of Versailles stripped Germany of its subject territories in Africa and the Pacific. In 1919, the League of Nations, dominated by the victorious Allied nations, granted the Union of South Africa a mandate to administer the territory of South West Africa as a trusteeship. The decision to relieve Germany of its colonial possessions was made easier through documents that attacked its rule and poor history with the native peoples, especially in the case of GSWA. Reports produced by Britain were especially effective in showing Germany incapable of stewarding and advancing its indigenous peoples. The so-called "Blue Book," published in 1919, described in detail how the Germans mistreated the Herero and Namaqua peoples during the 1904-1908 uprisings.[2] Decried as propaganda by the Germans, all the copies were later ordered destroyed in order to restore good relations between Germany and Britain following the 1925 Treaty of Locarno.[3] The die was nevertheless cast.

South West Africa under its new rulers looked little different to the native peoples than it had under the Germans. Many Germans, civilians and military veterans alike, remained in the territory and continued their lives much as before, while Afrikaners moved north to take advantage of newly available ranch land. It was the indigenous people who gained little from the change and, as before, became restive under continued white rule.

In 1917, Mandume Ya Ndemufayo, the last king of the Kwanyama peoples, was killed for his failure to recognize South African rule.[4] It was the beginning of a trend that would last 73 years.

The South African administration in Windhoek had as little tolerance for dissent as their predecessors. The Administration initially tended towards military solutions to resolve those problems, which were many. Racial prejudices continued, as did tax practices that guaranteed indigenous peoples, like the Bondelwarts and Rehoboth Basters, would be forced into the labor market to survive. While the mandate from the League of Nations prohibited slavery and forced labor, all the South African rules and laws that suppressed

---

1   John Dugard, *The South West Africa/Namibia Dispute: Documents and Scholarly Writings on the Controversy between South Africa and the United Nations*, p.27.

2   The full title is *Report on the Natives of South-West Africa and Their Treatment by Germany*.

3   Although accurate in detail, the "Blue Book" is still seen by many Germans as a propaganda piece meant to relieve Germany of its colonies in order to safe guard Britain's empire.

4   The cause of his death is disputed; South African records state he was killed by gunfire, while popular history attributes his death to suicide. See Patricia Hayes "Order out of Chaos: Mandume Ya Ndemufayo and Oral History", *Journal of Southern African Studies*, Vol. 19, No 1, pp.89-113.

its own black and Indian populations were enforced. Land issues that deprived locals of access to grazing acreage and benefitted white ranchers – both Afrikaners and Germans – contributed greatly to a hopelessness that drove many to despair and disobedience.

In 1922, the Bondelswarts, a clan of the Namaqua group, threatened to rise up against its new masters when their grievances where not addressed. The threat of violence and preparations for that uprising were answered with police raids, military operations, and aerial bombardment. The airplane that helped South Africa to victory in 1915 was now used as a tool of oppression and a weapon of terror against the populace.

The Basters also believed their lot would change with the new government. Their 1915 revolt against the Germans was predicated on the hope of being granted an independent homeland in return for services rendered. Baster leader Nels van Wyk had called on his people to abrogate their protection treaty with Germany in keeping with General Botha's alleged promise "that which you have, at least, you will keep." After the war, the Baster push for self-administration was denied and their resulting uprising was suppressed as well.[5]

Following the creation of the United Nations (UN) in 1946, South Africa refused to recognize a revision of the League of Nations mandate that required international supervision of their administration of the territory. Throughout this period, South Africa demonstrated that it intended to incorporate SWA into South Africa as a province, although it never officially carried that intent out. South African administration of SWA continued to be marked by demonstrations of power and punitive retributions against the indigenous peoples, who were thoroughly segregated from the white minority.[6]

Uprisings began again in 1959 with the deportation of blacks and coloureds from the capital Windhoek to a township called "Katutura." On 10 December 1959, police killed 11 and wounded 44 people who were protesting the move. This incident sparked events that would lead to the Namibian War for Independence, a struggle which paralleled events in South Africa that would eventually further inflame a war in Angola and end Apartheid .

The United Nations would revoke South Africa's Trusteeship (not observed by South Africa in any event) for SWA in 1966. Namibia would achieve independence in March 1990 after a protracted struggle fought mostly from outside its borders with the assistance of Cuba, the Union of Soviet Socialist Republics (USSR), East Germany and, to a lesser extent, the People's Reublic of China (PRC). For the ruling South West Africa People's Organization (SWAPO) and its supporters, that struggle and victory defined Namibia, its peoples, and politics.

Today, World War I is but a distant memory for most Namibians; a conflict fought by outsiders over a land taken from its true owners. Ultimately, Africans of all colours and creeds will determine the preservation of this historical legacy; like the country's future, both now belong to Namibians.

---

5   Andries Marius Fokkens, *The Role and Application of the Union Defense Force in the Suppression of Internal Unrest, 1912-1945*, p.75.

6   Although never with the level of violence and brutality that marked the German occupation.

Appendix I

Chronology

1652   Dutch East India Company (VOC) establishes Cape Colony. Britain occupies the colony in 1795 and again in 1806 to prevent the French from taking control. The colony remains under direct British control until 1872 when it became self-governing.

1883   Adolf Lüderitz purchases the harbor and surrounding land of Angra Pequena from the local Nama chief and establishes a trading post, which later becomes Lüderitzbucht (Lüderitz Bay).

1884
Apr 21   The territory of German Southwest Africa (GSWA) is established as a protectorate of Germany. The colony is administered by the private *Deutsche Kolonialgesellschaft für Südwest-Afrika* (German Colonial Society for Southwest Africa) then, after 1890 by the *Reichs Kolonial-Abteilung* (Imperial Colonial Department). After 1907, this became the *Reichskolonialamt* (Imperial Colonial Office).

1889
Apr 16   Establishment of *die Kaiserlichen Schutztruppe* (the Imperial Protection Force) as an internal security force in GSWA.

1910
31 May   Establishment of the Union of South Africa as a dominion of the United Kingdom.

1912
1 Jul   Union Defense Force is established by The Defense Act No. 13 of 1912.

1913   German Governor Theodor von Seitz and *Schutztruppe* Commander Lieutenant Colonel Joachim von Heydebreck make plans for mobilization (*Mobilmachung*) to defend the colony and a possible offensive against South Africa in preparation for war. The railway network is critical to that plan.

1914
Jan   Industrial Crisis and mobilization of Union Defense Force against strikers at mines in South Africa.

Aug 4/5 Telefunken Radio Station at Nauen, Germany sends "War with England, France, and Russia." The First World War begins. Union of South Africa Prime

Minister Louis Botha cables London suggesting the withdrawal of British forces from South Africa and offers to "defend" South Africa unilaterally. Botha realizes this is an opportunity to incorporate the German colony into South Africa.

Aug 6   Great Britain accepts Botha's offer and requests South Africa consider it undertake the capture of the wireless stations in GSWA as "a great and urgent Imperial service." Botha gathers cabinet political support for a military expedition against GSWA.

Aug 6-8   GSWA placed on war footing by Governor von Seitz. The active strength of the *Schutztruppe* is 1,967 men. General mobilization is ordered, and with a call-up of 3,000 reservists and *Landwehr*, the *Schutztruppe* increases to around 4,900 men.
           The Colonial Office of the Foreign Ministry in Berlin naively assures colonies "they are not in danger."

Aug 6   Governor von Seitz issues his guidance for the defense of GSWA.

Aug 8   Last German steamships depart Swakopmund for safe haven in South America.

Aug 10   The South African cabinet agrees to send an expedition against GSWA with two conditions: Parliamentary approval and the use of an all-volunteer force. Botha will have a total force of nearly 70,000 men at his disposal.

Aug 21   Border skirmish at Nakob between German troops and Afrikaaner farmers assists South African Prime Minister General Louis Botha in his efforts to rally support for military operations against the Germans.

Sep 10   The Union Parliament votes to adopt a motion of support for the King and to support all necessary measures to cooperate with the Imperial Government "to maintain the security and integrity of the British Empire."

Sep 12/13 The Union's "Force A" under Brigadier General H "Tim" Lukin enters German territory to begin offensive operations against GSWA. Lukin's forces capture the border town of Ramansdrift.

Sep 14   British Royal Navy ship *Armadale Castle* shells Swakopmund, wrecking the Customs House and several homes in an unsuccessful attempt to destroy the wireless station.

Sep 15   Several senior South African Boer officers resign their commissions in protest over the war with Germany. A number of Boers go over the border to offer their services to Germany. The *Vrijkorps* (Free Corps) is formed of Boers living in GSWA.

Sep 18/19   Union "Force C" under Colonel PS Beves lands at Lüderitzbucht consisting of one six-gun artillery battery, a squadron of the Imperial Light Horse, the Transvaal Scottish, the Rand Light Infantry and a section of engineers, sailed from Cape Town, make an uncontested landing.

Sep 21   Schuckmannsburg and the eastern Caprivi Strip occupied by a small contingent of British South Africa Police (BSAP) and Northern Rhodesia Police (NRP).

Sep 23   General Botha takes supreme command of Union operations against German South-West Africa.
Dismantling of the State railway between Swakopmund and Nonidas begins.

Sep 24   German forces under Captain Oscar Scultetus attack British enclave of Walvis Bay.
British warship *Kinfauns Castle* shells Swakopmund in retaliation.

Sep 26   German forces under Heydebreck overwhelm South African advance force at Sandfontein. After a 10-hour battle, 242 men, two artillery pieces, three machine guns, and supplies are captured.

Sep 30   British warship *Kinfauns Castle* again shells Swakopmund.

Oct 7/9   Union Colonel S.G. "Mannie Maritz contacts the Germans and goes into open rebellion against the South African Government. Rebellion spreads throughout Orange Free State and the Transvaal.

Oct 20   Germans dismantle first 32 kilometers of *Otavibahn* (OMEG) from Swakopmund.

Oct 26   Flight Lieutenant Paul Fiedler conducts aerial reconnaissance south to Steinkopf in South Africa. German forces raid into South Africa and destroy rail line between Steinkopf and Port Nolloth.

Nov 12   Heydebreck killed in accidental explosion of a rifle grenade during test firing at Kalkfontein-Süd. He is succeeded by Victor Franke as commander of the *Schutztruppe*.

Dec 22   Maritz's attack into South Africa fails despite having initially achieved surprise.

Dec 25   Landing of Northern Force under command of Colonel Skinner, consisting of one Mounted Regiment, two Infantry Brigades, and the Artillery Brigade (seven guns) at the British enclave of Walvis Bay.

1915

Jan 13	Swakopmund is occupied by South African forces; Germans abandon town and retire to the East. Major Wehle ordered to delay South African advance but not to attack Swakopmund. South Africans begin construction of a new rail line from Walvis Bay to Swakopmund. This line will be General Botha's supply lifeline for his advance into GSWA.
Jan 13/24	Maritz again crosses border but attack on Upington fails.
Jan 31	German supporting attack towards Steinkopf in South Africa, attack Kakamas instead; attack miscarries.
Feb 2	Botha arrives in Walvis Bay (with his wife) and takes command of all forces in GSWA and directly orchestrates the operations of Northern Force.
Feb 11	South Africans complete the railway from Walvis Bay to Swakopmund.
Feb 20	South Africans begin to rebuild *Otavibahn* to Cape Gauge (3'6") standard.
Feb 23	South Africans begin advance to Rössing and Heigamchab, 20 kilometers East of Swakopmund. Union forces occupy Goanikontes.
Mar 18	The Union main force departs Nonidas and marches 35km to Husab Camp; they arrive at Husab morning of 19 March.
Mar 19	Evening – Botha splits his force into two elements and moves east towards Riet with one, while the second element moves northeast towards Pforte. Union Scouts engage German forward observation post at Husab Pforte. UDF Lieutenant Uys is killed.
Mar 20	Union Forces attack Pforte and Jakalswater with one brigade under Colonel Alberts, while attacking Riet with a second brigade under Colonel Brits. About 30,000 Union troops advance from the South under General MacKenzie (Central Force from Lüderitzbucht), Colonel J. van Deventer (Southern Force from Steinkop), and Colonel Berrange (Eastern Force from Bechaunaland).
Apr 1	Botha meets Baster Captain Cornelius van Wyk in Swakopmund. Wyk allegedly receives Botha's support for a rebellion against the Germans. Botha denies giving any encouragement.
Apr 15	Rehoboth-Baster uprising begins at Rehoboth.
Apr 19	Germans retreat from Keetmanshoop in south.
Apr 23	Battle at Gibeon results in heavy losses for Germans. Germans continue

withdrawal from south and reach Rehoboth 90 kilometers south of Windhoek on 2 May 1915.

Apr 26   German Forces under Major Ritter attack the Union railhead at Trekkopje (Trekkoppies). First use of armored cars in Africa helps blunt the attack and Germans retire from the field after six hours of combat.

Apr 30   Battle of Otjimbingwe – Botha continues his advance up the Swakop River Valley with about 39,000 troops.

May 1   Capital of GSWA shifted from Windhoek to Grootfontein.

May 8   Battle of Sam-Kubas between Rehoboth-Bastards and German forces. Germans withdraw from the battle as Union forces approach area. Germans reach Waterberg on 13 May 1915.

May 12   Windhoek occupied by South Africans.

Jun 1   The battle at Otavifontein is fought between 800 Germans and 3,700 South Africans.

Jun 4   The last skirmish during World War One in GSWA is fought at Ghaub.

Jun 9   The German *Schutztruppe* surrender at KM 500 near Khorab on the *Otavibahn* rail line.

Jun 15   South West African Protectorate declared by the Union of South Africa.

Distribution of Forces at Pforte, Riet, and Jakalswater

March 19/20 1915

German Order of Battle – *"Kommando Rechte Flügel"*
Major Wehle ausser Dienst (Retired)

Total:	ca .700 Officers and Men
	12 Artillery Pieces

Jakalswater
"Regiment Naulila"	Captain Trainer (ca. 30 rifles)
Wachkommando – 2. Replacement Company	(15 rifles)
Signal Station on Walfischrucken	(2 men)

Modderfontein
1st Mountain Gun Battery *"Batterie Munstermann"*	Major Erno v. Munstermann"
Infantry Platoon	Lieutenant Sinn (50 rifles)

Riet
"Kustenregiment"	Captain Krüger (200 rifles)
2. Infantry Company *"Kompanie Ohlenschlager"*	Captain Ohlenschlager
2. Company	Captain Freiherr von Watter
3. Reserve Battery *"Batterie Haußding"*	Captain Haußding
Machine-gun Platoon (3 x guns)	Lieutenant Rosenow
Infantry Platoon	Lieutenant Tesch
Heliograph Signal Station	Lieutenant Halsbrand

Pforte
6. Company *"Kompanie Weiß"*	Captain Weiß (190 rifles)
2. Replacement Company *"Kompanie Steffen"*	Lieutenant Steffen (33 rifles)
"Halb Batterie Weiherr"	Senior Lt Hans v. Weiherr
Observation Post (OP)	Lieutenant Bötticher
Machine-gun Platoon (2 x guns)	
Signal Station (Heliograph / Telephone)	Sergeant Pater (3-4 rifles)
Observation Post	Sergeant Sanio (10 rifles)

Heavy Weapons (total)

1st Mountain-gun Battery	4 x 7.5 cm L/14 M. 08
3rd Reserve Battery	6 x 7.7cm FK96 n/A[1]
Half Battery "*Weiherr*" (captured at Pforte)	2 x 7.7cm FK96 n/A
Machine-guns	5 x Maxim 7.92mm MG-08

Union Defense Forces Order of Battle – Northern Force
General Officer Commanding (GOC) Louis Botha

Total:	ca. 7,500 Officers & Men
	14 Artillery Pieces

Right Wing (at Pforte and Jakalswater)

2nd Mounted Brigade	Colonel J.J. Alberts
	(2,600 rifles)
2nd Brigade Right Wing	Colonel Commandant L.J. Badenhorst
	(1,311 rifles)
Heidelburg A. Cdo.	
Standerton B. Cdo.	
Swart's Scouts (15th Intelligence Unit)	
Ermelo A. Commando (Cdo)	
Standerton A. Cdo.	Commandant Piet Botha
Heidelburg B. Cdo.	
4th Permanent Field Artillery (PFA)	
2 sections Imperial Light Horse w/ MGs	Major Giles
2 Brigade Left Wing	Colonel Commandant W.R. Collins
	(1,253 rifles)
Bethal Cdo.	
Carolina Cdo.	
Ermelo B. Cdo.	
Middelburg A. Cdo.	
Middelburg B. Cdo	
Collin's Scouts (16th Intelligence Unit)	

Left Wing (at Riet)

1st Mounted Brigade	Colonel Coen Brits
(2,300 rifles)	Major Brink

---

1   Some sources state the 3rd Res Battery was equipped with FK 96 a/A (old model) guns, but archival and photographic evidence shows it had the newer FK 96 n/A guns at Riet, four of which were equipped with splinter shields. The battery's original guns (FK 96 a/A) were turned over to the *Freikorps* in December 1914, after which it was equipped with newer pieces.

1st Brigade Right Wing

Colonel Commandant
Piet de la Rey
(1,089 Rifles)

Krugersdorp Cdo.
Potchefstroom A. Cdo.
Potchefstroom B. Cdo.
de la Rey's & Oosthuizwn's Scouts (13th Intelligence Unit)
Uys's Scouts

1st Brigade – Left Wing

Colonel Commandant
L.A.S. Lemmer
(1,200 rifles)

Bloemhof Cdo.   Commandant Bezuidenhout
Lichtenburg Cdo.
Marico Cdo.
Wolmaranstad Cdo.
Grobler's Scouts
Lemmer's Scouts (14th Intelligence Unit)
Transvaal Horse Artillery (THA) Battery
General Botha's Bodyguard   Major Harry Trew
(100 Rifles)

General Reserve under the control of GOC Botha
Rand Rifles
Durban Light Infantry (posted to JKW after battle)
One Machine Gun Section (ILH)
One Heavy Artillery Battery
One Heavy Artillery Section
Section of 2nd Mounted Brigade (horses judged to be unfit for duty)

Heavy Weapons

Transvaal Horse Artillery	4 x QF 13-pdr Guns
Permanent Field Artillery	4 x QF 13-pdr Guns
Hvy Artillery Bat	2 (?) x QF 12-pdr 18 cwt guns*
Hvy Artillery Section	2 (?) x QF 4.7-inch guns*
H1 Battery	1 x Armstrong BLC 15 pdr AA Gun**
Machine-guns	Unknown Number of Maxim .303 caliber

* With General Reserve / Line of Communications Troops.
** A second Armstrong AA gun was with MacKenzie's forces at Tschaukaib as H2 Battery.

Appendix III

The Fallen

South African Personnel Killed in Action during the Swakop River Valley Campaign

Name	Rank	Place / Unit	Date
Allen T	Sig	Swakopmund / NTC	14.1.15
Anderson WE	Pte	Trekkopje / 7 IKR	26.4.15
Branfield HE	Pte	Unknown / So. Rifles	28.5.15
Breytenbach HJ	Cpl	Riet/Pforte / MCdo	20.3.15
Burnett GM	Pte	Walvis Bay / ILH-5MR	21.1.15
Cameron TA	Cpl	Trekkopje / 7 IKR	26.4.15
Cameron Wm	Lt	Trekkopje / 8 IKR	26.4.15
Cook J	Bgr	Unknown / WtbCdo	16.5.15
De Meyer WA	Bgr	Riet/Pforte / E Cdo	20.3.15
Dempers HJ	Lt	Unknown / USct	8.4.15
Dyke ESC	Pte	Walvis Bay / 5MR	21.5.15
Engelbrecht AAJ	Bgr	Unknown / MCdo	30.4.15
Filer DA	Cpl	Trekkopje / 7 IKR	26.4.15
Harrison F	Capt	Trekkopje / 7 IKR	26.4.15
Jacobs PJ	Bgr	Pforte / 1 MB	20.3.15
Jooste FPJJ	Bgr	Riet-Pforte / KCdo	20.3.15
Lambie A	Pte	Trekkopje / 7 IKR	26.4.15
Levine C	Sgt	Jakalswater / KCdo	20.3.15
Mey JA	Bgr	Jakalswater / ECdo	20.3.15
Meyer FW	Bgr	Riet-Pforte / PtCdo	20.3.15
Nel JP	SM	Riet-Pforte / ECdo	20.3.15
Reid GS	Pte	Trekkkopje/ 8 Inf	26.4.15
Sacks B	Tpr	Unknown / BCdo	6.4.15
Seyffert WJ	Bgr	Riet-Pforte / PtCdo	20.3.15
Van Den Berg JD	Bgr	Unknown / PCdo	1.5.15
Van Den Heever JO	Bgr	Unknown / PCdo	30.4.15
Van Der Hoven FH	SSM	Riet-Pforte / MCdo	20.3.15
Van Rebsburg JHC	Bgr	Karibib / PCdo	10.5.15
Van Tonder WM	Bgr	Riet-Pforte / CCdo	20.3.15
Venter AJ	Bgr	Unknown / MCdo	30.4.15
White EB	Bgr	Unknown / BCdo	16.4.15
Wills JR	Cpl	Trekkopje / 7 IKR	26.4.15
Uys JN	Lt	Riet-Pforte / WCdo	19.3.15

1st Rhodesian Regiment Personnel Killed in Action

Name	Rank	Place / Unit	Date
Clayton C.C.W.F.	Pte	Swakopmund	7.2.15
Rabinson B.	Pte	Swakopmund	7.2.15
Hollingsworth F	Lt	Trekkopje	26.4.15

South African Unit Abbreviations

1 MB	1st Mounted Brigade
5 MR	5th Mounted Regiment
7 IKR	7th Inf Kimberley Regiment
8 IKR	8th Inf Kimberley Regiment
8 Inf	8th Infantry
NTC	Natal Telegraph Corps
ILH	Imperial Light Horse
USct	Uys Scouts
BCdo	Bloemhof Commando (Cdo)
CCdo	Carolina Cdo
ECdo	Ermelo Cdo
KCdo	Krugersdorp Cdo
MCdo	Middelburg Cdo
PCdo	Pietersburg Cdo
PtCdo	Potchefstroom Cdo
WCdo	Wolmaranstad Cdo
WtbCdo	Waterburg Cdo

South African / Rhodesian Rank Abbreviations

Pte	Private
Bgr	Burgher
Bdr	Bombadier
Rfn	Rifleman
Tpr	Trooper
Cpl	Corporal
Sig	Signalman
Sgt	Sergeant
Const	Constable
QMS	Quarter Master Sergeant
SM	Sergeant Major
SSM	Staff Sergeant Major
BSM	Brigade Sergeant Major
RQMS	Regimental Quarter Master Sergeant
Adj	Adjutant
Lt	Lieutenant
Capt	Captain
Cmdt	Commandant
Maj	Major

German Personnel Killed in Action During the Swakop River Valley Campaign

Name	Rank	Place / Unit	Date
Aßmann, Albert	Uffz d. R	Pforte / 6 K	20.3.15
Bechler, Josef	Reiter d. Ldst	Pforte / HalbBteW	20.3.15
Ewald, Walter	Lt. d. Ldst	Pforte / 2 EK	20.3.15
Einicke, Paul Emil	Gefr. d. Ldst	Trekkopje / 2 RK	26.4.15
Göhring, Alfred	Gefreiter	Pforte / 6 K	20.3.15
Hepach, Hoemanns	Sanitäter VizFdw	Riet / 2 K	20.3.15
Happ, Jozef	Gefreiter	Pforte / 6 K	20.3.15
Haase	Gefreiter	Trekkopje / 2 K	26.4.15
Klein	Gefreiter	Trekkopje / 2 RK	26.4.15
Kosmala, Johann	Reiter	Pforte / 6 K	20.3.15
Kranz, Hermann	Reiter	Pforte / 6 K	20.3.15
Krafft, Kurt	Gefr d. Ldst	Trekkopje	26.4.15
Lüders, Albert	Uffz. d. Ldst	Riet / 2 IK	20.3.15
Marquardt	Reiter d. R	Trekkopje / 2 RK	26.4.15
Müller, Ludwig	Lt d. R	Trekkopje / 2 RK	27.4.15
Mikolaizack, Stanislaus	Gefr d. Ldst	Pforte / HalbBteW	20.3.15
Pater, Franz	Sergeant	Pforte / 6 K	20.3.15
Peper, Max	Gefreiter	Pforte / HalbBteW	20.3.15
Pichen	Gefreiter	Trekkopje / 2 K	26.4.15
Raub, Josef	Reiter d. Ldst	Pforte / 2 EK	29.5.15
Schiemann, Otto	Gefreiter d. R	Pforte / 6 K	20.3.15
Schmidt, Hans	Reiter Kfw	Riet / 2 IK	20.3.15
Schoer	Reiter d. Ldst	Salem / 2 IK	21.3.15
Senf	Reiter Kfw	Trekkopje / 2 K	27.12.15
Thale	Gefreiter	Riet / 3 R Bte	20.3.15
v.Watter, Wilhelm Frhr	Hauptmann	Trekkopje / 2 K	26.4.15
Waldner	Uffz d. Ldst	Trekkopje / 2 RK	26.4.15
v.Weiher, Hans	Oblt d. R	Pforte / HalbBteW	20.3.15
Weber, Willie	UZahlmeister	Jakalswater	20.3.15
Wille, Hermann	Uffz d. Ldst	Riet / 2 IK	20.3.15
v.Wangeheim, E. Frhr	VizFeldw. d. R	Pforte / 6 K	20.3.15
Waldner, Karl	Uffz d. Ldst	Trekkopje / 2 RK	26.4.15

German Unit Abbreviations

2 K	2nd Company
2 EK	2nd Replacement Company
2 IK	2nd Infantry Company
2 RK	2nd Reserve Company
3 RBte	3rd Reserve Battery
6 K	6th Company
HalbBteW	Artillery Half Battery von Weiher

German Rank Abbreviations

Reiter	Trooper
Reiter d. Ldst	Trooper Home Defense (*Landsturm*)
Reiter Kfw	Trooper Volunteer (*Kriegsfreiwilliger*)
Gefreiter	Corporal
Gefreiter d. R	Corporal of the Reserves
VizFeldw. d. R	Staff Sergeant of the Reserve
VizFeldw. d. Ldst	Staff Sergeant of the Home Defense (*Landsturm*)
Sergeant	Sergeant
Uffz d. Ldst	Non-commissioned Officer of the Home Defense (*Landsturm*)
Uffz d. R	Non-commissioned Officer of the Reserve
Lt. d. Ldst	Lieutenant of the Home Defense (*Landsturm*)
Lt d. R	Lieutenant of the Reserves
Oblt. d. R	Senior (1st) Lieutenant of the Reserves
Hauptmann	Captain
Sanitäter VizFdw	Medical Vice Sergeant
UZahlmeister	Junior Paymaster

Sources and Bibliography

Archival Materials

Botswana National Archives (BNA), Gabarone.
RC 11/1, Reports to the Foreign Office, Subject: Herero.
RC 11/2, Correspondence of the Regional Commissioner, Subject: Herero.
Namibian National Archives (NNA), Windhoek.
A.0560, BArch NL 30, Victor Franke, *Tagebuch: 1896-1920*, unpublished manuscript, 13 volumes.
STR 1/1/25, *Einleitung – Inventar der Akten der Kaiserlichen Schutztruppe: 1896-1914*, [Introduction to the Inventory of the Imperial Protection Force Files: 1896-1914], FJ Kutzner.
ZBU 2372, IX.e-l, *Geheimakten: Kommandeur – ST Mobilmachungvorarbeiten*, [Secret Files: Commander – Preparations for Mobilization of the Protection Force].
National Archives and Records Administration (NARA), Washington DC.
Record Group 59, *Zimmermann Telegram, Decoded Message*, General Records of the Department of State, 1756 – 1979,
The National Archives, (TNA), Kew.
WO 106, WO 181, WO 33, *Despatches of Col FJA Trench*, War Office Files.
FO 367, *Despatches from FT* [Frederick Trench], Foreign Office File.
FOL 1907, *Foreign Office List for 1907*, Foreign Office File.
Western Cape Archives, Cape Town.
PMO 227, Ref 35/07, *German South West Africa – Supplementary Estimates and Policy -Reports From British Embassy, Berlin, 1907*, Prime Minister's Office File.

Printed Books and Articles

Baden-Powell, Robert, LTG Sir, *Aids to Scouting*, London: Gale & Polden, 1915.
Baericke, Max, *Naulila: Errinerungen eines Zeitgenossen*, Swakopmund: Gesellschaft für Wissenschäftlichen Entwickelungen und Museum, 1981.
Barfield, Doreen, "The Battle of Trekkoppies," *South African Military History Society, Military History Journal*, Vol 2, No 2, Dec 1971.
Bayer, Maximilian, *Mit dem Hauptquartier in Südwestafrika*, Berlin: Wilhelm Weicher, 1909.
Botha, Louis, quoted in "The South African Defense Act." *The Morning Post*, 2 Jul 1912, quoted in *Scientiae Militaria*, Vol 28, Issue 2, Sep 1998.
Callwell, C.E., *Small Wars: Their Principles & Practice*, 3rd ed, Lincoln: University of Nebraska Press, 1996.
Chanock, Martin, *Unconsummated Union: Britain, Rhodesia and South Africa, 1900-1945*, Manchester: Manchester University Press, 1977.
Churchill, Winston, *My Early Life: 1874-1904*, New York: Scribner, 1996.
Clayton, Anthony, *Forearmed: A History of the Intelligence Corps*, London: Brassey's, 1993.
Collyer, J.J., *The Campaign In German South West Africa*, Pretoria: Government Printer, 1937.

Collyer, J.J., "Mounted Rifle Tactics," *Military Journal*, Apr 1915, pp 265 – 305.

Dugard, John, *The South West Africa/Namibia Dispute: Documents and Scholarly Writings on the Controversy between South Africa and the United Nations*, Berkeley: University of California Press, 1973.

Dorning, W.A., "A Concise History of the South African Defense Force (1912-1987)," *Scientia Militaria, South African Journal of Military Studies*, Vol 17, No 2, 1990, pp.1-24.

Farwell, Byron, *The Great War in Africa, 1914-1918*, New York: WW Norton & Company, 1989.

Fergusson, Thomas G, *British Military Intelligence 1870-1914*, Frederick, MD: University Publications of America, 1984.

Fokkens, Andries Marius, "The Role and Application of the Union Defense Force in the Suppression of Internal Unrest, 1912-1945", Masters Thesis, Stellenbosch: Stellenbosch University, 2006.

George, David Lloyd, *War Memoirs*, London: Nicholson & Watson, 1933.

Grimes, Shawn T, *Strategy and War Planning in the British Navy, 1887-1918*, Woodbridge: The Boydell Press, 2012

Hayes, Patricia, "Order out of Chaos: Mandume Ya Ndemufayo and Oral History", *Journal of Southern African Studies*, Vol. 19, No. 1, Special Issue: Namibia: Africa's Youngest Nation, Mar 1993, pp.89-113.

Hennig, Richard, Rittmeister, *Deutsch-Südwest im Weltkrieg*, Wolfenbuttel: Melchior, 2011.

Haupt, Werner, *Deutschlands Schutzgebiete in Übersee 1884-1918*, Wölfersheim: Podzun-Pallas Verlag, 1984.

Jacobs, André, Lt Col, and Cdr Hennie Smit, "Topographic Mapping Support In The South African Military During The 20th Century," *Scientia Militaria, South African Journal of Military Studies*, Vol 32, Nr 1, 2004, pp.32-50

Keene, J.L., "The Problem of Munitions Supply in the First World War and its effect on the Union Defense Force," *South African Military History Society, Military History Journal*, Vol 6 No 4, Dec 1984.

Kinahan, John, and Stejskal, James, "Finding Europe's Great War in Africa," *Current World Archaeology*, Number 59, pp.48-51.

Kinahan, John, "QRS Job 106: Assessment of historical site on proposed Otjikoto-Ohorongo 132kV power-line," Windhoek: Quaternary Research Services, 2012.

Kinahan, John, "QRS 157: Archaeological field survey of a site for the proposed Arandis Thermal Power Generation and Waste Oil Recycling Plant," Windhoek: Quaternary Research Services, 2012.

Kraus, Jürgen, and Müller, Thomas, *Die deutschen Kolonial- und Schutztruppen von 1889 bis 1918: Geschichte, Uniformierung und Ausrüstung*, Vienna: Verlag Militaria, 2009.

Kriegsgeschichtlichen Abteilung I des Großen Generalstabes (KA I), *Die Kämpfe der deutschen Truppen in Südwestafrika*, First through Sixth Books in Two Volumes. Berlin: Hofbuchhandlung, 1906/1907.

Kriegsgeschichtliche Forschungsanstalt des Heeres (KFH), *Der Feldzug in Deutsche Südwestafrika, 1914-1915, (Entwurf)*, Potsdam: 1943.

L'Ange, Gerald, *Urgent Imperial Service: South African Forces in German South West Africa, 1914-1915*, Rivonia: Ashanti, 1991.

"Left Arm," *The Action at Trekkopje – A Day of Lost Opportunities for the PBI in South West Africa*, Cape Town: Springbok, 1915.

Leipoldt, Major J.G.W., DSO, report on operations in German South West Africa submitted to the War Office by the South African Government, available at http://www.kaiserscross.com/41992/home.html.

Lenssen, H.E., *Chronik von Deutsch-Südwestafrika: 1893-1915*, Windhoek: Namibia Wissenschaftliche Gesellschaft, 2008.

von Lettow-Vorbeck, Paul Emil, *My Reminiscences of East Africa*, Uckfield: Naval and Military Press, undated.

von Lettow-Vorbeck, Paul Emil, *Heia Safari! Deutschlands Kampf in Ostafrika*, Leipzig, Hase & Koehler, 1920.

Mahncke, J.O.E.O., "Aircraft Operations in the German Colonies: 1911-1916 – The Fliegertruppe of the Imperial German Army," *South African Military History Society, Military History Journal*, Vol 12 No 2, Dec 2001.

Mantei, Sebastian, "Von der „Sandbüchse" zum Kommunikationsnetzwerk: Die Entwicklungsgeschichte des Post- und Telegraphenwesens in der Kolonie Deutsch-Südwestafrika (1884 – 1915)", PH.D Dissertation presented before Martin-Luther-Universität, Halle-Wittenberg, 2004.

McGregor, Gordon, *Das Burenfreikorps von Deutsch-Südwestafrika*, 1914-1915, Windhoek: Namibia Wissenschaftliche Gesellschaft, 2010.

McLaughlin, Peter, *Ragtime Soldiers: the Rhodesian Experience in the First World War*, Bulawayo: Books of Zimbabwe, 1980

Mohlamme, J.S., "Soldiers Without Reward: Africans in South Africa's Wars," The South African Military History Society, *Military History Journal*, Vol 10 No 1, Jun 1995.

Moore, Ritchie, *With Botha in the Field*, London: Longmans, Green & Co., 1915.

Nortier, Erasmus Wentzel, "Major General Sir Henry Timson Lukin (1860-1925): The Making Of A South African Hero," Master's Thesis presented to University of Stellenbosch, 2005.

von Oelhafen, Hans, *Der Feldzug in Südwest 1914 – 1915*, Berlin: Safari Verlag, 1923.

Olusoga, David and Casper W. Erichsen, *The Kaiser's Holocaust: Germany's Forgotten Genocide and the Colonial Roots of Nazism*, London: Faber & Faber, 2010.

Oosthuzen, G.J.J., "The Military Role Of The Rehoboth Basters During The South African Invasion Of German South West Africa, 1914-1915," in *Scientia Militaria, South African Journal of Military Studies*, Vol 28, Nr 1, 1998.

Paice, Edward, *World War I: The African Front: An Imperial War on the Dark Continent*, New York: Pegasus Books, 2008.

Paterson, Hamish, "First Allied Victory: The South African campaign in German South-West Africa, 1914-1915," *The South African Military History Society, Military History Journal*, Vol 13 No 2 – Dec 2004.

Pattee, Phillip, "A Great and Urgent Imperial Service: British Strategy for Imperial Defense during the Great War, 1914-1918," Doctoral Dissertation: Temple University, 2010.

Proppe, Gregor, Dr, *Erinnerungen eines sehr alten Tieratztes*, Meppen: Buchdruckerei Huer and Klass, 1920.

Rayner, W.S. & W.W. O'Shaugnessy, *How Botha & Smuts Conquered German South West*, privately published, 1915.

Remak, Joachim, *The Origins of World War I, 1914-1918*, New York: Holt, Rinehart, and Winston, 1967.

Rust, H.J., Dr, "Aus meinem Leben," *Newsletter of the South West African Scientific Society*,

Issue XIX/I, Windhoek: SSSWA, 1978.

Samson, Anne, Britain, *South Africa and the East African Campaign, 1914-1918: The Union Comes of Age*, London: I.B. Taurus, 2005.

Schepp, Sven, *Unter dem Kreuz des Südens: Auf Spuren der Kaiserlichen Landespolizei von Deutsch-Südwestafrika*, Frankfurt am Main: Verlag für Polizeiwissenschaft, 2010.

Scotland, Alexander P., LTC, *The London Cage*, London: Evans Brothers, 1957.

von Seitz, Theodor, *Südafrika im Weltkriege*, Berlin: D. Reimer, 1920.

Seifert, Karl D, *Flieger über den Kolon*ien, Zweibrücken: VDM Heinz Nickel, 2007.

Seligmann, Matthew, "A View From Berlin: Colonel Frederick Trench and the Development of British Perceptions of German Aggressive Intent, 1906-1910," *The Journal of Strategic Studies*, Vol. 23, No. 2 (June 2000), pp.114-147.

Seligmann, Matthew, *The Royal Navy and the German Threat 1901-1914: Admiralty Plans to Protect British Trade in a War Against Germany*, Oxford: Oxford University Press, 2012.

Seligmann, Matthew, *Spies in Uniform: British Military and Naval Intelligence on the Eve of the First World War*, Oxford: Oxford University Press, 2006.

Seligmann, Matthew, *Rivalry in Southern Africa: The Transformation of German Colonial Policy*, London: Macmillan, 1998.

Strachan, Hew, *The First World War in Africa*, Oxford: Oxford University Press, 2004.

Steinmetz, George, *The Devil's Handwriting: Precoloniality and the German Colonial State in Qingdao, Samoa, and Southwest Africa*, Chicago: University of Chicago Press, 2007.

Union Defense Force (UDF), *South Africa in the Great War 1914-1918: Official History*, originally published 1924, reprinted, Nashville: The Battery Press, 2004.

Union of South Africa, *Report on the Natives of South-West Africa And Their Treatment By Germany*, London: HMSO, 1918.

van der Waag, Major I.J., "Major J.G.W. Leipoldt, DSO: A Portrait of a South African Surveyor and Intelligence Officer, 1912-1923," *Scientia Militaria*, Vol 25, No 1, 1995, pp.12-34.

van der Waag, Ian, "The battle of Sandfontein, 26 September 1914: South African military, reform and the German South-West Africa campaign, 1914–1915, *First World War Studies*, DOI: 10.1080/19475020.2013.828633.

Walker, Henry Francis Bell, *A Doctor's Diary in Damaraland*, London: Arnold, 1917.

Warwick, Rodney C, "The Battle Of Sandfontein: The Role And Legacy Of Major General Sir Henry Timson Lukin," [article on-line], accessed 12 Dec 11, available at http://www0.sun.ac.za/sdorm/index2.php?option=com_docman&task=doc_view&gid=29&Itemid=26, Internet.

Whitthall, W, Lt Cdr, *With Botha and Smuts in Africa*, London: Cassell & Co., 1917.

Index

Lightning Source UK Ltd.
Milton Keynes UK
UKOW06f1249120416

272089UK00004B/119/P